Fancy Dress
for Girls & Boys

Fancy Dress for Girls & Boys

JEAN GREENHOWE

B.T. Batsford, London

ISBN 0 7134 5516 0

Typeset by Servis Filmsetting Ltd, Manchester
and printed in Great Britain by
R.J. Acford Ltd
Chichester, Sussex
for the publishers
B.T. Batsford Ltd
4 Fitzhardinge Street
London W1H 0AH

Contents

Introduction

The following pages show how to make nursery tale and historical fancy dress for children up to 142 cm (4 ft 8 in.) in height. The eighteen outfits are put together using only the most basic of sewing skills and if you can gather, stitch seams and turn hems, then you will be able to make everything in this book.

Instead of complicated patterns, full use is made of rectangular and circular shapes which are quick and easy to draw out from the measurements given. Any other pattern shapes are kept as simple and uncomplicated as possible and clear diagrams are given for these.

In addition, the step-by-step instructions are written in such a way as to cover the exact size you require, at each stage of making. For this reason, the book should be especially useful for anyone faced with the costuming of a stage production, which involves children of different sizes.

In some cases, items of everyday clothing can be used as a basis for the costume and only a couple of specially-made garments need to be added.

The simple techniques which are described in detail, will provide endless possibilities for designing many more fancy dress outfits and with a little ingenuity, the costumes could easily be adapted to fit adults.

General Instructions

These should be read before starting to make any of the costumes.

The quantities of materials required

For convenience, the amounts of materials required are given for height 142 cm (4 ft 8 in.). If the costume is to be made for a smaller child, then any savings on these amounts can be calculated by first reading through the instructions. The most obvious example of this is in the *length* of a garment, where, for a smaller child, you would need less than the amount stated.

Fabrics

Curtain and soft furnishing fabrics, in general, are especially good for making fancy dress costumes for children, since they are usually woven in broader widths than dress fabrics and this makes it possible to cut some of the garments in one piece.

Remnants of these fabrics, which are too small for making curtains, can also be picked up quite cheaply in the sales.

There is a non-woven type of curtaining which is inexpensive and extremely useful for making costumes. This fabric is firm and has good 'body' rather like felt, and the cut edges need no finishing off as they do not fray. It can be obtained in a variety of widths and a range of bright self-colours. Refer to the photograph of Friar Tuck to see what this fabric looks like.

The cheaper types of curtain brocades look very luxurious when used for fancy dress, but extra care should be taken when handling the pieces after cutting out, as the raw edges tend to fray easily.

An old sheet will provide a valuable quantity of fabric for making such things as underskirts, shirts, blouses and aprons etc.

It is also worth while searching in thrift shops and jumble sales, where second-hand curtains, net curtains and bed linen can all be found at a fraction of the cost of new fabric by the yard. You should also look out for bargain-priced evening dresses in luxury fabrics such as satin or lurex, as these can be cut up and used for fancy dress. There may even be a few suitable items of cast-off clothing in your own household.

Any second-hand goods should be washed and ironed and the garments unpicked or cut apart at the seams, before using.

Decorative trimmings

These can be quite expensive to buy by the yard, but attractive trimmings can also be found on garments in thrift shops and jumble sales. You may pay only a few pence for an item of clothing trimmed with several yards of lace, ribbon, sequins, or braid etc., which would cost a few pounds if bought new. It takes time to unpick of course, but the saving is worth while. Buttons, snap fasteners and zips etc., can also be salvaged.

Stiffening collars, hats etc.

Firm interlining such as heavy-weight Vilene, is ideal for stiffening hats and collars. Two types of this interlining are available, iron-on and sew-in. The instructions throughout the book are given for the sew-in type and when two or more layers are needed, these have to be stuck together, by applying spots of glue here and there. However, if you buy the iron-on type, the layers can be fused together, following the manufacturer's instructions.

Making the patterns and cutting out

In the instructions, there are measurements for all the simple shapes required, such as circular or rectangular pieces. Other patterns are given as diagrams with measurements. You will need a ruler (imperial or metric) or, better still, a yard stick, for drawing long straight lines. If you don't have a yard stick, then use a long, straight strip of rigid cardboard or piece of wood.

Draw the patterns from the measurements given on the diagrams, onto large sheets of brown wrapping paper or newspaper. You can use an ordinary pair of school compasses for drawing small circles, but for many of the garments, large circular patterns are required and these can be drawn in the following way.

First of all, fold a square of paper of sufficient size into quarters. Tie a pencil to one end of a length of string near to the pencil point. The string should be longer than the required radius of the circle to be drawn. Note that the radius of a circle is *half* the diameter (the measurement across the centre). Measure the length of the radius along the string from the pencil point, keeping the string taut, then tie a knot in the string at this point. Place a drawing pin through the knot and into the folded corner of the square of paper.

Now draw the quarter circle as shown in the diagram, keeping the string tightly stretched and holding the drawing pin in place at the same time. Cut along the drawn line through all the layers of paper, then unfold, to give the full size pattern.

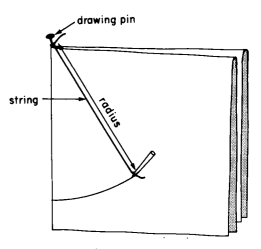

Drawing out large circles

When a pattern is marked along one edge 'place to fold', this means to place the edge to a fold in the fabric, so that the piece can be cut from double thickness.

The patterns for the frog prince are printed full size and should be traced off the page onto thin writing paper.

The one-piece tunic pattern

This pattern is extremely versatile and can be adapted in a number of ways. Once you have taken the time to draw the pattern from the diagram, it can be used to make a number of the costumes in the book and will certainly spark off ideas for many more.

Although the measurements are given in detail on the tunic diagram, absolute accuracy is not essential, as a little extra or less will make no difference.

The task of drawing the pattern full size can be made easy if you use dressmakers' graph paper. This paper is marked into 1 cm ($\frac{3}{8}$ in.) squares, with heavier lines at 5 cm (2 in.) intervals and you would only need to count the squares, following the measurements given. The graph paper can be bought from haberdashery and fabric shops.

Since this tunic is so useful, it is a good idea to make it up using an oddment of fabric, such as old sheeting. It can then be tried on the child to see if any adjustments may be necessary, before cutting the actual costume fabric. This can also be invaluable when making several outfits for children of different sizes.

The one-piece pants pattern

This should be drawn out in the same way as the tunic pattern, to the size you require. Although it is only needed for two of the costumes in the book, it is a useful pattern to have on hand, if you should decide to try out your own costume ideas.

Sewing equipment

You will need the usual sort of equipment for ordinary household sewing, such as a sewing machine, sewing thread, pins, needles, large scissors and a tape measure etc.

Sewing and gluing

1.3 cm ($\frac{1}{2}$ in.) seams are allowed on all pieces unless otherwise stated.

Join all pieces with right sides together and press seams open after sewing, unless other instructions are given.

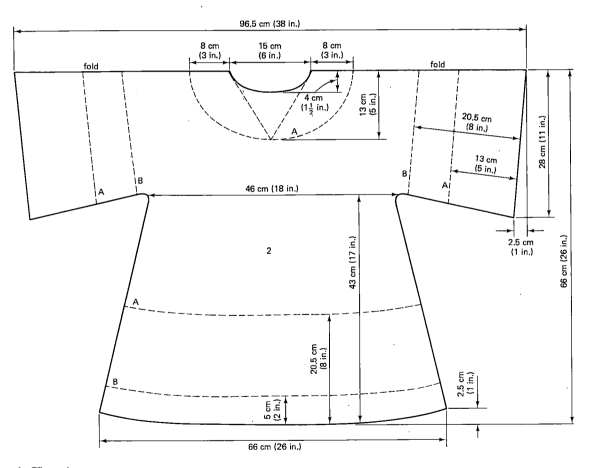

1. *The tunic pattern.*

The raw edges of seams may be finished off by overlocking if your machine has a zig-zag facility, otherwise you can oversew by hand. This is not essential, but it will prevent the raw edges from fraying and make the garment last longer.

When adhesive is quoted in the instructions this should be an all-purpose clear adhesive such as UHU, which is colourless and dries very quickly. Glue is sometimes used to hold fabric or interlining pieces together before they are sewn and you only need to apply a few spots here and there.

To draft out the tunic pattern, use a sheet of brown wrapping paper or dressmaker's graph paper measuring at least 66 cm by 96.5 cm (26 in. by 38 in.). Alternatively, smaller sheets can be stuck together with sticky tape to give the required size. Fold the sheet of paper in half as shown in diagram 2 and draw on the tunic to the sizes given in diagram 1, halving the measurements across the width of the pattern. Cut out the pattern, then mark on all the other lines shown on the tunic pattern.

When cutting out the tunic from fabric, always place the top edge marked 'fold' to a fold in the fabric as shown in diagram 3. After sewing the underarm and side seams of the tunic, clip the fabric at the underarm curves as shown in diagram 4 so that the seams will not wrinkle when the tunic is turned right side out.

When the tunic hem edge or the sleeves have to be cut to a shorter length for a particular garment, the excess pieces can be cut off the pattern and laid aside. After cutting the tunic from fabric, the pieces can be stuck back on to the pattern with sticky tape. In the same way extra length can be added on to the sleeve and hem edges.

To draft out the pants pattern:

Measurements are given for this pattern to be drawn out in three sizes. The smallest size is given first, then the medium and larger sizes follow in brackets. If in doubt about which size to use for the child, check the various measurements against a pair of ordinary trousers or pyjama pants which fit the child.

On a sheet of brown wrapping paper or dressmaker's graph paper measuring at least 30.5 cm by 92 cm (12 in. by 36 in.) draw out the pants pattern to the measurements given in diagram 1. Cut out the pattern.

Cut out two pants pieces from fabric, each time placing the edge marked 'fold' against a fold in the fabric. Join the two pants pieces to each other at the centre edges as shown in diagram 2. Bring

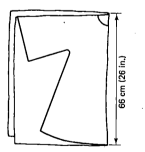

2. *Fold the sheet of paper in half and draw the tunic pattern as shown.*

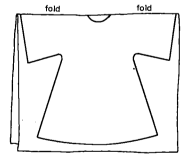

3. *Cut the tunic from double fabric placing the upper edge against the fold.*

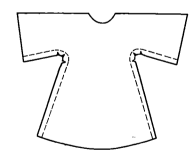

4. *Clip the side and underarm seams in the underarm curves.*

1. *The pants pattern.*

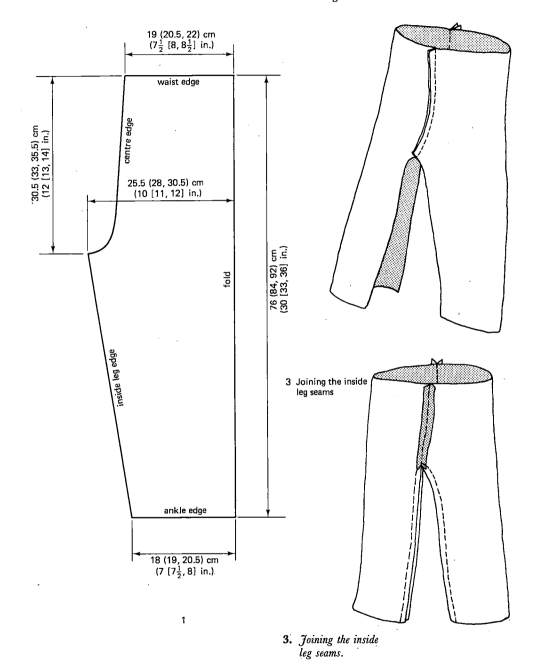

19 (20.5, 22) cm
(7½ [8, 8½] in.)

waist edge

centre edge

30.5 (33, 35.5) cm
(12 [13, 14] in.)

25.5 (28, 30.5) cm
(10 [11, 12] in.)

fold

76 (84, 92) cm
(30 [33, 36] in.)

inside leg edge

ankle edge

18 (19, 20.5) cm
(7 [7½, 8] in.)

1

2. *Joining the centre edges.*

3 Joining the inside leg seams

3. *Joining the inside leg seams.*

these seams together and join the inside leg seams as shown in diagram 3. Turn in and hem the ankle edges. Hem the waist edge, taking a 4 cm ($1\frac{1}{2}$ in.) turning to form a casing for the elastic. Thread the elastic through to fit the child's waist.

Robin Hood

This is a quickly-made fancy dress using green non-woven curtain fabric for the tunic and hood.

Tights and sweater

These can be green, brown or fawn.

Ankle boots

Use a pair of brown knee socks a few sizes larger than the child's foot. Turn the socks inside out and sew the toe ends to a pointed shape as shown in diagram 1. When turned right side out, the socks can be worn on top of gym shoes or slippers, rolling the tops down around the ankles.

1. *Sewing the toe ends of the socks to a point.*

Tunic and Hood

Materials required for height 142 cm (4 ft 8 in.)

1.4 m (1½ yd) of 122 cm (48 in.) wide green curtain fabric.
5.1 m (5½ yd) of plain braid for edging the tunic and hood; alternatively, bias binding can be used.

Two buttons and a shoe lace for the fastening on the hood.

To make the tunic

Use the tunic pattern given on page 9, shortening the sleeve and lower edges to the lines marked B. Place the pattern against the child to check that the hem edge comes slightly lower than the tops of the legs, then shorten or lengthen the pattern as necessary.

Cut the tunic from fabric as shown in diagram 2. Then cut out the V-neckline on the front of the tunic only, as shown on the tunic pattern. Join the underarm and side seams and clip the underarm curves. Try the tunic on the child to see if larger turnings need to be taken on these seams to make the tunic fit neatly. Sew braid or bias binding to the neck, sleeve and hem edges to cover the raw edges.

To make the hood

This hood will fit all sizes. Draw out the hood pattern as shown in diagram 3, beginning by drawing out a quarter circle with a 51 cm (20 in.) radius. Mark on the other dotted lines to the measurements given, then cut out the pattern. Cut the hood from fabric as shown in diagram 2, then join the back edges leaving the lower curved edge and the face edge open. Sew on braid or bias binding to cover these raw edges. Sew a button to each side of the hood at the neckline, then make a small loop from the shoe lace and twist it around the buttons to fasten as illustrated.

Belt and quiver

Materials

A belt.
Small pieces of leather cloth and cardboard for the quiver.
Adhesive.

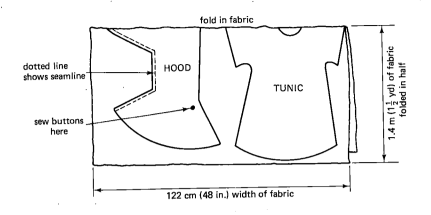

fold in fabric

dotted line
shows seamline

HOOD

TUNIC

sew buttons
here

1.4 m (1½ yd) of fabric
folded in half

122 cm (48 in.) width of fabric

2. *Cutting out the*
tunic and hood.

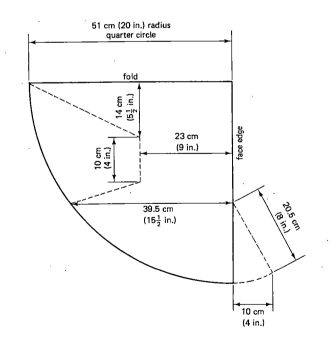

51 cm (20 in.) radius
quarter circle

fold

14 cm
(5½ in.)

23 cm
(9 in.)

face edge

10 cm
(4 in.)

39.5 cm
(15½ in.)

20.5 cm
(8 in.)

10 cm
(4 in.)

3. *Making the hood pattern.*

15

To make the quiver

Make the quiver pattern as shown in diagram 4, then cut out two pieces from leather cloth. Join the pieces together, taking 0.3 cm ($\frac{1}{8}$ in.) seam and leaving the top edges open. Turn right side out. To stiffen the quiver, cut two pieces of cardboard using the quiver pattern, then trim 0.6 cm ($\frac{1}{4}$ in.) off all the edges. Place the pieces of cardboard inside the quiver, one at the front and one at the back. Then fold the top edges of the leather cloth to the inside and glue to the cardboard.

Cut 1.3 cm ($\frac{1}{2}$ in.) wide strips of leather cloth and glue these around the quiver as shown in diagram 4. Sew two loops of leather cloth to the back of the quiver to hang it on the belt as illustrated.

Bow and arrows

Use a toy bow and arrows.

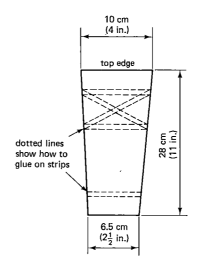

4. *The quiver.*

17

Friar Tuck

This costume is quick and easy to make using non-woven brown curtain fabric. To give Friar Tuck the necessary stoutness of figure, a couple of extra sweaters or an anorak should be worn underneath the tunic. A small circle of pink felt moulded to shape is used for the tonsure, the bald patch on the head, and this can be fixed to the child's hair with hair grips.

Tunic and collar

Materials required for height 142 cm (4 ft 8 in.)

2.8 m (3 yd) of 122 cm (48 in.) wide brown non-woven curtain fabric.
46 cm ($\frac{1}{2}$ yd) of narrow elastic.

To make the tunic

Use the tunic pattern given on page 9, lengthening the sleeve edges to make full length sleeves, and lengthening the hem edge so that it will reach to the child's ankles. A little extra should also be allowed on the side and underarm seams to give more fullness if the tunic is for an older child.

Cut the tunic from fabric as shown in diagram 1. The sleeve edges can be taken to the full width of the fabric, and this extra can be folded back if the sleeves are too long for the child, as shown in the illustration. Cut out the rounded neck edge a little lower than given on the tunic pattern.

Join the underarm and side seams and clip the underarm curves. Clip the neck edge at intervals, then hem the neck, sleeve and lower edges.

To make the collar

Draw out the collar pattern as shown in diagram 2. This collar will fit all sizes. Cut two collar pieces from fabric as shown in diagram 1, then join the pieces at the sides leaving the top and lower edges open. Hem the top and lower edges, then thread elastic through the top edge to draw it in slightly. When the collar is worn, turn the top edge to the inside, forming folds as shown in the illustration.

Girdle

For the girdle use 1.9 m (2 yd) of very thick cotton piping cord. This can be dyed brown.

Sandals

Any kind of strap sandals can be used. Alternatively, to make the sandals as shown in the illustration, cheap plastic flip-flop sandals are used. Remove the toe straps and replace them with long brown boot laces, lacing these around the feet and ankles as shown in the illustration.

19

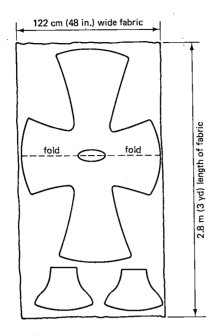

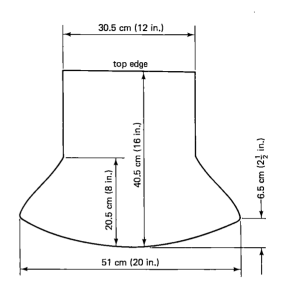

122 cm (48 in.) wide fabric

fold   fold

2.8 m (3 yd) length of fabric

30.5 cm (12 in.)

top edge

40.5 cm (16 in.)

20.5 cm (8 in.)

6.5 cm (2½ in.)

51 cm (20 in.)

1. *Cutting out the tunic and hood pieces.*

2. *The collar pattern.*

Tonsure

For this, use a 15 cm (6 in.) diameter circle of pink felt. Soak it thoroughly in a strong solution of starch, then ease it over the base or the inside of a small pottery bowl to give the correct shape to fit the child's head. Allow to dry, placing the bowl in a warm oven if desired to speed up the drying process. When the felt is dry, glue four short lengths of tape inside the circle close to the outer edge, leaving a gap at the centre of each tape unglued through which a hair grip can be slipped, as shown in diagram 3.

3. *Showing how to fix the tapes inside the tonsure.*

Stick

Friar Tuck carries a stout stick. For this a suitable straight branch cut from a tree can be used, or a length of wooden dowelling.

20

Miss Mufffet

This outfit is made from thin curtain fabrics, using flower printed nylon for the dress and hat, and plain coloured net with frilled edges for the shawl top and lower sleeves. A long nightdress could be used instead of making the dress; then only the shawl top, hat and spider would have to be specially made.

Dress and hat

Materials required for height 142 cm (4 ft 8 in.)

3.2 m (3½ yd) of 92 cm (36 in.) wide printed nylon curtain fabric.
2.8 m (3 yd) of 92 cm (36 in.) wide fabric for lining the dress, or cuttings from an old sheet.
92 cm (1 yd) of 82 cm (32 in.) wide firm interlining for the hat brim.
1.6 m (1¾ yd) of 92 cm (36 in.) wide plain net fabric with ready frilled edges.
92 cm (1 yd) of 5 cm (2 in.) wide ribbon for the belt.
46 cm (½ yd) of narrow ribbon in the same colour as the belt.
5 cm (2 in.) of Velcro for the belt fastening, or hooks and eyes can be used instead.
56 cm (22 in.) length of narrow elastic.
Adhesive.

To make the dress

Use the tunic pattern given on page 9, altering it as follows: shorten the sleeve edges to the lines marked A, then cut out the neck edge along the line marked A. Lengthen the hem edge of the pattern so that the tunic is just above ankle length on the child. The pattern width requires no alteration as the belt, gathered sleeve edges and elasticated neck edge ensure that the dress will fit all sizes.

Cut out the tunic shape and hat pieces from printed fabric as shown in diagram 1. Join the side and underarm seams of the dress, then clip the underarm curves. Hem the lower edge, then turn the dress right side out. Cut out the tunic shape from the lining fabric, join the underarm and side seams in the same way as for the dress, then hem the lower edge. Turn the lining right side out and place it inside the dress. Tack the raw neck and sleeve edges of the lining and dress together, then bind the neck edge with bias strips of dress fabric and thread the narrow elastic through.

Cut out the pieces from the frilled edged net fabric as shown in diagram 2. To make the lower sleeves, pin each of the sleeve pieces, right side inside, around the child's arms as shown in diagram 3, having the 30.5 cm (12 in.) length of the fabric along the length of the arms, and

1. *Cutting out the dress and hat pieces.*

2. *Cutting out the frilled edged net pieces.*

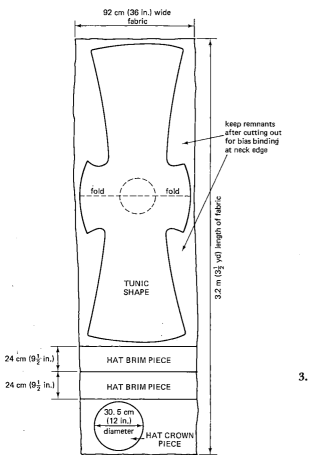

92 cm (36 in.) wide fabric

keep remnants after cutting out for bias binding at neck edge

fold   fold

TUNIC SHAPE

3.2 m (3½ yd) length of fabric

24 cm (9½ in.)   HAT BRIM PIECE

24 cm (9½ in.)   HAT BRIM PIECE

30. 5 cm (12 in.) diameter   HAT CROWN PIECE

92 cm (36 in.) wide fabric

SHAWL TOP

92 cm (1 yd)

1.6 m (1¾ yd) length of fabric

LOWER SLEEVE   LOWER SLEEVE

25.5 cm (10 in.)

30.5 cm (12 in.)   30.5 cm (12 in.)

keep remnants for dress hem frill and hat band

3. *Pinning the sleeve fabric to fit around the arm.*

pinning the fabric loosely enough so that the sleeves can be pulled off the arms easily. Pull the sleeves off and sew the seams as pinned then trim off the excess fabric close to the seams.

Gather the raw sleeve edges of the dress to fit the upper raw edges of the plain net sleeves, then stitch them in place.

Cut the ribbon for the belt to the child's chest size just beneath the arms, plus 2.5 cm (1 in.) for an overlap. Sew the Velcro or hooks and eyes to the overlap.

For the shawl top, fold the 92 cm (1 yd) length of plain net fabric in half, bringing the two frilled edges together. Tie a length of strong thread tightly around the centre of the strip as shown in diagram 4 and pin this tied centre to the outside of the belt at the centre front. Place the belt on the

4. *Showing shawl top folded in half with one end gathered.*

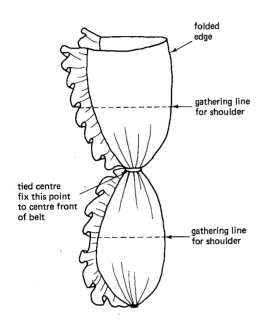

folded edge

gathering line for shoulder

tied centre
fix this point
to centre front
of belt

gathering line for shoulder

5. *Cutting a section out of the brim shape.*

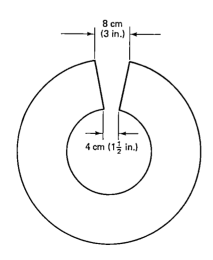

8 cm
(3 in.)

4 cm (1½ in.)

child, then take each side of the shawl piece back over each shoulder. Gather up each end of the shawl piece and pin inside the belt on either side of the overlap fastening. Sew the ends in place where they are pinned. Now run a gathering thread through the fabric along each shoulder, drawing up the gathers as necessary to make the shawl top fit on the shoulders as shown in the illustration. Fasten off the gathering threads. Make a bow from the narrow ribbon and sew it to the centre front as illustrated.

Make a frill from strips of the remaining plain net fabric and sew the frill to the dress hem.

To make the hat

For the hat brim, cut out four 40.5 cm (16 in.) diameter circles from the piece of interlining, then from the centre of each one cut out an 18 cm (7 in.) diameter circle and discard it. Cut a section out of each brim shape as shown in diagram 5. Glue all the brim pieces together.

To cover the brim, join the two 24 cm by 92 cm (9½ in. by 36 in.) pieces of dress fabric together to make a 24 cm by 184 cm (9½ in. by 72 in.) length. Fold this strip in half along the length with right sides outside, then stitch the long edges together, taking 0.6 cm (¼ in.) seam. Slip this tube of fabric on to the brim shape, with the seam at the inner edge of the brim. Space out the pleats of fabric evenly. Overlap the short edges of the brim shape 0.6 cm (¼ in.) and stitch, then turn in the remaining short raw edges of the tube of fabric and slip stitch them together so that the brim is completely covered.

For the crown of the hat, use the 30.5 cm (12 in.) diameter circle of dress fabric and also cut out a 30.5 cm (12 in.) diameter circle of lining fabric. Place the pieces together with the right sides uppermost, then run a gathering thread round the edge through both thicknesses. Pull up the gathers so that the crown will fit the inner edge of the brim. Sew the crown in place, taking 0.6 cm (¼ in.) seam and spacing out the gathers in the crown evenly. Cut a strip of the left-over plain net fabric and tie it round the hat for a hat band, holding it in position with a stitch here and there.

Shoes and socks

Ballet shoes or slippers can be worn with coloured socks to match the dress fabric.

Bowl and spoon

Use a plastic bowl and spoon in a colour which matches the dress fabric.

The spider

Materials

Small piece of brown velvet or felt for the body.
Scrap of white felt and two sequins for the eyes.
Cotton wool for stuffing.
Length of yarn or thin string for the legs.
Adhesive.

To make

Cut a 9 cm (3½ in.) diameter circle of velvet or felt and run a gathering thread around the edge. Put a little stuffing in the centre of the circle and pull up the gathers slightly. Continue adding more stuffing until the body is a firm rounded shape. Pull the gathering thread tight and fasten off. This gath-

6. *Showing positions of legs on spider.*

ered side is the underside of the spider.

Cut two ovals of white felt for the eyes, measuring about 0.9 cm by 1.6 cm (⅜ in. by ⅝ in.) Glue these in position, then glue on sequins as shown in diagram 6.

For the legs, cut four 11.5 cm (4½ in.) lengths of yarn or string. Using a darning needle take each length through from one side of the body to the other, spacing them out evenly and leaving equal lengths of yarn protruding at each side to form eight legs. Spread glue on all the legs, allow it to become tacky, then bend the legs into shape as shown in diagram 6.

For the spider's thread, use a short length of silvery thread if possible, taking it through from the underside of the spider to the top of the head with a darning needle. Tie a knot in the end of the thread underneath the body and attach the other end of the thread to the edge of the hat brim, as shown in the illustration.

Spanish Costume

A plain red sleeveless T-shirt with a low neckline is the basis for the bodice of this dress, but one with short sleeves would also be suitable. Matching cotton seersucker fabric is used for the skirt and the sleeve frills. Red striped or checked fabric could be used instead.

Dress

Materials required for height 142 cm (4 ft 8 in.)

5.5 m (6 yd) of 92 cm (36 in.) wide cotton fabric.
A plain T-shirt which matches the cotton fabric.
14 m (15 yd) of white trimming, this can be lace edging, ric-rac braid or white tape etc.
2 hooks and eyes.
15 cm (6 in.) of Velcro.

To make the skirt

For the basic skirt, cut two 35.5 cm by 92 cm (14 in. by 36 in.) strips of fabric. Note that for smaller sizes the 35.5 cm (14 in.) measurement should be the child's measurement from the hip to above the knee. Join the short edges of the strips leaving a 10 cm (4 in.) gap at the top of one seam for the centre back opening of the skirt. Gather the upper edge to fit the child's hip measurement plus 2.5 cm (1 in.).

For the hem frill, cut four 40.5 cm by 92 cm (16 in. by 36 in.) strips of fabric. Note that for smaller sizes the 40.5 cm (16 in.) measurement should be the measurement from the lower edge of the basic skirt to just above the ankles. Join the strips together at the short edges forming a continuous piece. Hem one long raw edge and sew on the white trimming. Gather the remaining long raw edge to fit the lower edge of the skirt and sew it in place.

For the top frill, cut three 25.5 cm by 92 cm (10 in. by 36 in.) strips of fabric. Make this frill a little narrower for smaller sizes. Make up and trim the frill in the same way as given for the hem frill. Gather the remaining long raw edge to fit the top gathered edge of the skirt and sew it in place having the raw edges even.

Cut out and make the middle frill in the same way as given for the hem frill. Gather the remaining long raw edge to fit the basic skirt and pin it in place about half-way up the skirt, positioning it so that the hem frill will be the widest, the middle frill a little narrower and the top frill the narrowest. Sew the gathered edge of the middle frill in place.

Bind the top raw edges of the skirt with a strip of lace edging or a strip of the cotton fabric. Sew hooks and eyes to the back overlap.

Cut the hooked side of the Velcro strip into 2.5 cm (1 in.) pieces and sew them inside the top edge of the skirt having one at each side, two evenly spaced at the front and two at the back. This is for fixing skirt to T-shirt when the dress is worn.

To make the bodice

Gather a 92 cm (1 yd) length of lace edging to fit the neck edge of the T-shirt and sew it in place. Alternatively, a narrow strip of cotton fabric may be used instead of lace edging.

For each sleeve, cut a 10 cm by 51 cm (4 in. by 20 in.) strip of cotton fabric. Join the 10 cm (4 in.) edges of each strip. Gather one long edge to fit the armhole or sleeve edge of the T-shirt and sew it in place.

For each sleeve frill, cut a 20.5 cm by 92 cm (8 in. by 36 in.) strip of cotton fabric. Join the 20.5 cm (8 in.) edges of each strip. Hem one long edge and sew on trimming. Gather the remaining raw edge to fit the sleeve and sew it in place.

Put the bodice on the child then put on the skirt. Mark the position of the Velcro strips on the T-shirt. Sew 2.5 cm (1 in.) pieces of the furry strip of Velcro to the T-shirt at the marked positions.

Socks and shoes

White socks and plain black shoes can be worn.

Hair and mantilla

The hair should be secured in a bun at the crown of the head. A comb is then fixed in to the bun. An ordinary side comb can be used for this but to give it extra height, glue on a strip of strong card folded in half as shown in diagram 1.

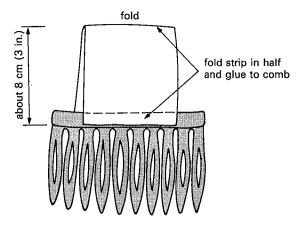

about 8 cm (3 in.)

fold

fold strip in half and glue to comb

1. *Gluing a piece of card to the comb to give it height.*

The lace mantilla may be black or white and either dress fabric or curtain lace is suitable. Fold in half, corner to corner, a 92 cm (36 in.) square of lace fabric to make a triangle. Note that if the fabric used is heavy it may be best to cut the lace fabric in half as folded and use only one triangular piece.

Drape the triangle of fabric over the comb having the longest edge of the triangle at the front edge of the hair. Catch the mantilla to the top edge of the comb with a few small stitches.

Accessories

Castanets, a tambourine or a fan can be carried.

Cinderella
and the
Fairy Godmother

Cinderella's cage of six small mice and the pumpkin make this an attractive outfit though it costs very little to make. Instructions are given here for the blouse and skirt, but a child's ordinary blouse and an adult's old cotton skirt could be used instead.

Skirt

Materials required to fit any size

Two strips of 92 cm (36 in.) wide cotton fabric the required length from waist to ankles.
A length of petersham ribbon about 2.5 cm (1 in.) wide, the child's waist measurement plus 8 cm (3 in.), for the waistband.
Velcro or hooks and eyes for the waistband fastening.
Scraps of bright printed fabrics for the patches.

To make

Machine stitch fabric patches all over the skirt pieces as shown in the illustration. Join the strips of skirt fabric at the sides, leaving a 15 cm (6 in.) gap at the top of one seam for the side opening. Gather up the waist edge to fit the child's waist and sew it to the length of ribbon. Sew Velcro or hooks and eyes to the waistband at the overlap. Cut the lower edge of the skirt into ragged points.

Blouse

Note that this blouse will fit all sizes because of the elasticated sleeve and neck edges.

Materials

92 cm (1 yd) of 82 cm (36 in.) wide brushed nylon fabric.
92 cm (1 yd) of narrow elastic.

To make

Use the tunic pattern given on page 9. Shorten the lower and sleeve edges to the lines marked A, then cut out the neck edge along the line marked A. Cut the blouse from the fabric.

Hem the sleeve and neck edges forming casings for the elastic. Thread elastic through the sleeve edges to fit the child's upper arms and sew the ends of the elastic in place at the ends of the casings.

Thread elastic through the neck edge to fit as illustrated.

Join the side and underarm seams, then clip the underarm curves. Hem the lower edge.

Belt

Materials

A 10 cm (4 in.) wide strip of felt long enough to go around the child's waist.
A strip of firm interlining the same size as the felt.
A long boot lace.

To make

Stitch the felt and interlining together all round about 1.3 cm ($\frac{1}{2}$ in.) from the edges. Trim a little off the edge of the interlining so that it will not show on the right side of the belt. Snip five small holes at even intervals in each of the short edges of the belt. Thread the boot lace through as shown in the illustration.

Scarf

Use a man's handkerchief.

Shoes

Cinderella can have bare feet, or wear gym shoes or slippers.

Cage of mice

Materials

A small lampshade frame. The one illustrated measures 11.5 cm ($4\frac{1}{2}$ in.) diameter at the narrow end, 14 cm ($5\frac{1}{2}$ in.) diameter at the other end by 11.5 cm ($4\frac{1}{2}$ in.) in height. It has six struts.

String, for making extra struts on the cage.
Small piece of card for the cage base.
Brown enamel paint.
Scraps of fleecy fabric or felt for the mice.
Cotton wool for stuffing.
Small black beads for eyes.
Pink felt for ears.
Yellow plasticine for the lump of cheese.
Adhesive.

To make

First remove any interior lamp fittings from the lampshade frame. Fill in the gaps between the struts and across the top by tying on lengths of string, keeping the string taut. Make a string loop at the top of the cage with which to carry it. Paint the entire cage with enamel paint and put it aside to dry.

Cut a circle of card to fit the bottom of the cage. Model the plasticine into a wedge shape and make round holes and scooped-out bits as though nibbled by the mice. Glue cheese to the card base.

For the mouse pattern use one quarter of a 10 cm (4 in.) diameter circle of paper. Cut out six mice from fleecy fabric or felt. Oversew the straight edges of each mouse piece together, turn right side out and stuff with a little cotton wool. Run a gathering thread round the remaining raw edge and pull up tightly, enclosing one end of a bit of string for a tail. Fasten off the thread.

Glue two tiny beads to each head for eyes about 1.3 cm ($\frac{1}{2}$ in.) from the pointed end. Mark the pointed end with black pen or pencil for the nose. Make the whiskers by taking a needle and double black thread through the face just behind the nose, then snipping the threads short on either side of the nose.

For the ears, cut 0.9 cm ($\frac{3}{8}$ in.) diameter circles of pink felt. Cut a small straight edge off each one and stick these edges in position behind the eyes.

Glue all the mice to the cage base around the cheese in various positions, as shown in the illustration. Then glue the edge of the base to the lower edge of the cage.

Pumpkin

Materials

A strip of yellow fabric 23 cm by 61 cm (9 in. by 24 in.).
Kapok for stuffing.
Small piece of green felt for the pumpkin stalk.
Strong nylon or other thread for tying around the pumpkin.
Adhesive.

To make

Join the 23 cm (9 in.) edges of the fabric strip, then gather up one of the remaining raw edges tightly and fasten off the thread. Turn right side out and stuff firmly. Gather up the remaining raw edge

1. Robin Hood and Friar Tuck

2. *Little Miss Muffet*

3. *Cinderella and the Fairy Godmother*

4. *The Queen and Knave of Hearts*

5. *The Queen of Hearts*

6. *The Knave of Hearts*

7. *The Frog Prince and Princess*

8. *Tudor Costume c 1530*

9. *Mary, Mary Quite Contrary*

10. *Victorian Evening Dress c 1850*

and fasten off the thread. The gathered edges form the top and base of the pumpkin.

To form the pumpkin 'sections', tie threads very tightly around the pumpkin, crossing them over at the top and base as shown in the illustration.

For the stalk, cut a 5 cm by 9 cm (2 in. by $3\frac{1}{2}$ in.) strip of green felt; snip one 9 cm ($3\frac{1}{2}$ in.) edge into points. Spread the strip with glue and roll it up along the length spreading out the points to glue to the top gathered point of the pumpkin. Glue stalk in place.

For a more realistic effect, paint streaks of green, white and yellow water paint on the pumpkin.

34

This costume could also be used for Cinderella in her ball dress or any other fairy tale princess.

Dress and hat

Materials required for height 142 cm (4 ft 8 in.)

3 m (3¼ yd) of 122 cm (48 in.) wide shiny curtain fabric.
4.4 m (4¾ yd) of silver braid or trimming.
2.3 m (2½ yd) of 92 cm (36 in.) wide transparent non-fray fabric or fine curtain net.
70 cm (¾ yd) of narrow elastic.
3.7 m (4 yd) of nylon ribbon.
Hooks and eyes or snap fasteners for the bodice fastening.
Two 35.5 cm (14 in.) squares of firm interlining for making the hat shape.
Small strip of Velcro for the wrist band fastenings.
Adhesive.

To make the dress

First make the bodice. Cut a strip of curtain fabric 25.5 cm (10 in.) wide, long enough to go around the child's chest plus 11.5 cm (4½ in.). Turn in the 25.5 (10 in.) edges 4 cm (1½ in.) and stitch. This will leave enough fabric for an overlap of 4 cm (1½ in.) at the back of the bodice. Place the bodice on the child, overlapping and pinning the back edges. Mark the positions of the underarms, then take the bodice off the child and cut out two shallow semi-circles at the marked underarm positions. Turn in the upper edges 1.3 cm (½ in.) and stitch, clipping the underarm curves.

For each shoulder strap, cut a 10 cm by 30.5 cm (4 in. by 12 in.) strip of fabric, fold along the length and sew the long edges together. Turn the straps right side out and press.

Put the bodice on the child with the right side of the fabric inside and overlap and pin the back edges. Pin the shoulder straps to the top edges to make the bodice fit neatly under the arms. Pin a dart in the fabric at each side of the bodice to make

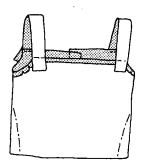

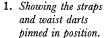

1. *Showing the straps and waist darts pinned in position.*

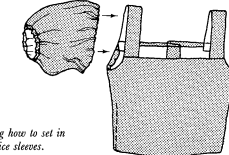

2. *Showing how to set in the bodice sleeves.*

it fit to the waist as shown in diagram 1. It may be necessary at this stage to cut the lower edge of the bodice to waist length if it is too long, but it should be left 1.3 cm (½ in.) longer than the child's waistline. Stitch the darts as pinned, then stitch the shoulder straps to the upper edge of the bodice at the front and back.

For each sleeve, cut a 20.5 cm by 51 cm (8 by 20 in.) strip of fabric. Hem one long edge of each sleeve piece to form a casing for the elastic. Thread elastic through to fit the child's upper arms, then sew the elastic in place at each end of the casing. Join the 20.5 cm (8 in.) edges of each sleeve piece.

Turn in the remaining raw edge of each sleeve and run a gathering thread through it. Slip stitch this edge to the shoulder strap and underarm curve as shown in diagram 2, pulling up the sleeve gathers to fit, and keeping most of the gathers at the top of the shoulder straps.

For the skirt, cut a strip of fabric 1.9 m (2 yd) long (join shorter lengths if necessary) by 61 cm (24 in.) wide. Note that for a smaller child, the width of this strip should be about two-thirds of the total skirt length from waist to floor level.

Join the short edges of the skirt strip, taking 4 cm (1½ in.) seam and leaving 15 cm (6 in.) open at the top of the seam for the back opening. Press the seam to one side.

For the skirt frill, cut 35.5 cm (14 in.) wide strips (or one-third of the total skirt length measurement) about 2.8 m (3 yd) or more in length, according to the amount of fabric available. Join up the frill strips, then gather one long raw edge to fit the lower edge of the skirt and sew it in place.

Gather the upper edge of the skirt to fit the lower edge of the bodice and sew it in place. Turn up and stitch the hem edge of the frill. Sew braid or trimming and a ribbon bow to the bodice and skirt as shown in the illustration. Sew hooks and eyes or snap fasteners to the back bodice overlap.

For the wings, cut a 1.9 m (2 yd) length of 92 cm (36 in.) wide transparent fabric. Fold it in half along the length, then in half again. Repeat this several times, then cut a scalloped shape through all thicknesses at one end so that when the strip is opened up again, it is evenly scalloped along one edge. Attach the centre of the other long edge to the centre back neck edge of the dress bodice with a few stitches.

Make wrist bands to fit the child's wrists from strips of braid, fastening them with strips of Velcro. Attach the ends of the wings to the wrist bands together with lengths of ribbon to hang down as illustrated.

To make the hat

For the hat, draw, then cut out two 35.5 cm (14 in.) radius quarter circles from the squares of interlining and glue them together. Spread a little glue all round the edges of the shape then place it on the wrong side of a piece of the left-over dress fabric. Cut out the fabric along the edges of the hat shape. Overlap and glue the straight edges of the shape about 0.6 cm (¼ in.) to form a cone shape, snipping about 2.5 cm (1 in.) off the top point in order to be able to do this.

Sew braid around the lower edge of the hat, then sew the remaining piece of transparent fabric and a length of ribbon to the top point. Sew each end of a length of elastic to the inside of the lower edge of the hat to hold it firmly on the child's head.

Underskirt

To make the dress skirt stand out well, an underskirt can be made from an old cotton sheet. Make it in the same way as the dress skirt, putting a little more fabric in to the frill if possible. Gather the waist edge on to a length of tape, leaving enough tape at each end for tying it around the waist.

Magic wand

Materials

A 51 cm (20 in.) length of thin wooden dowelling.
A star-shaped Christmas decoration.
Silver sticky tape.
Adhesive.

To make

Cover the dowelling by winding sticky tape around it, then glue the star to one end. Tie a bow of ribbon left over from making the dress, to the wand.

Hot Cross Buns

Instructions are given here for making all the items of clothing, but ordinary pants, a shirt or sweater, and socks could be used as a basis. If ordinary pants are used, the legs should be made to fit close-to the child's legs by running a strong tacking thread parallel to the outside leg seam. The pants legs should then be turned up on the inside to make them just reach to the calf of the leg. A pair of old pants could also be altered permanently by cutting off the excess leg length. The hot cross buns are easy to make from felt and old nylon tights or stockings.

Striped socks

These are made from a piece of stretchy striped towelling. For one sock cut a 30.5 cm (12 in.) wide piece of towelling long enough to reach from the child's toe to well above the knee. The stripes should go around the leg. Pin the strip around the child's leg and foot with the right side of the fabric inside as shown in diagram 1, stretching the towelling to fit neatly as it is pinned on. This stretching process will shorten the sock so that it will reach just to the knee. Pull off the sock and stitch the seam as it is pinned. Trim off the excess fabric close to the seam. Hem the upper edge and thread through a length of elastic to fit the leg. Turn right side out and make another sock in the same way.

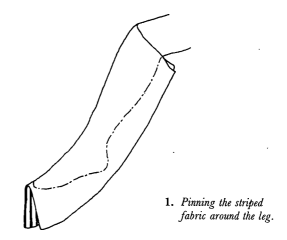

1. *Pinning the striped fabric around the leg.*

Buckled shoes

Black gym shoes are used with a metal buckle sewn to the front of each one. The tongues are made from felt stiffened by gluing it to thin card. Sew the centre bar of each buckle to each shoe. Cut the felt tongues to the correct width for threading through the buckles, making them wider at the top as shown in diagram 2. Thread the tongues through the buckles, then put a dab of glue at the back of the buckles to hold the tongues in place.

37

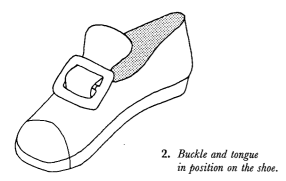

2. *Buckle and tongue in position on the shoe.*

Shirt and hat

Materials required for height 142 cm (4 ft 8 in.)

1.9 m (2 yd) of 92 cm (36 in.) wide white fabric, or cuttings from an old sheet.
46 cm (½ yd) of narrow elastic.
30 cm (⅜ yd) of 82 cm (32 in.) wide firm white interlining.

To make the shirt

Use the tunic pattern given on page 9, shortening the sleeve edges to the lines marked B and shortening the lower edge to the line marked A. Cut the shirt from white fabric, then cut out the rounded neck edge about 1.3 cm (½ in.) lower than given on the tunic pattern.

Join the underarm and side seams and clip the underarm curves. Try the shirt on the child to see if larger turnings should be taken on these seams for a neater fit. Check also that the sleeve edges do not come too far down the arms, though they should come well off the shoulders for the dropped shoulder effect. Cut a little off the sleeve edges if necessary, then measure the distance from this edge to the child's knuckles. Cut a strip of fabric this length by 56 cm (22 in.) wide for each sleeve.

Fold each sleeve strip in half and join the edges which form the length of the sleeves. On each sleeve gather one 56 cm (22 in.) edge to fit the sleeve edge of the shirt and sew it in place. Gather the remaining 56 cm (22 in.) edges to fit the wrists loosely, then bind these raw edges with bias strips of fabric.

Bind the neck edge with a bias strip of fabric and thread through elastic to fit the neck. Hem the lower edge of the shirt.

To make the hat

Cut two 15 cm (6 in.) wide strips of interlining long enough to go round the child's head plus 1.3 cm (½ in.). Glue them together. Overlap the 15 cm (6 in.) edges 1.3 cm (½ in.) and sew in place. To cover this tube shape, cut a 20.5 cm (8 in.) wide strip of fabric the same length as the interlining strip. Join the 20.5 cm (8 in.) edges taking 0.6 cm (¼ in.) seam. Turn right side out and place this tube over the interlining tube so that one raw edge and one edge of the interlining are even. The fabric tube will be 5 cm (2 in.) longer than the interlining tube at the other end as shown in diagram 3. Turn this raw edge of the fabric to the inside and stitch it to the edge of the interlining. Now turn up the remaining fabric which extends beyond the interlining tube to form a cuff as shown in diagram 4.

For the hat crown, cut a 51 cm (20 in.) diameter circle of fabric. Turn in the edge 0.6 cm (¼ in.) and run a gathering thread around it. Place the gathered circle right side out over the tube and pull up the gathers to fit. Sew the gathered edge to the outside of the tube about half-way down, as shown in diagram 4.

Pants

Materials required for height 142 cm (4 ft 8 in.)

92 cm (1 yd) of 122 cm (48 in.) wide non-woven curtain fabric.
70 cm (¾ yd) of 2.5 cm (1 in.) wide elastic.
Six buttons

3. *The tube shape for the hat.*

4. *Sewing on the hat crown.*

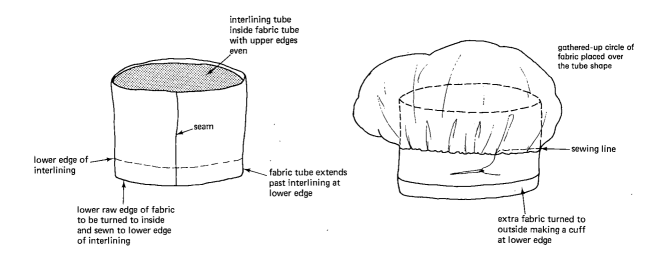

interlining tube inside fabric tube with upper edges even

seam

lower edge of interlining

fabric tube extends past interlining at lower edge

lower raw edge of fabric to be turned to inside and sewn to lower edge of interlining

gathered-up circle of fabric placed over the tube shape

sewing line

extra fabric turned to outside making a cuff at lower edge

To make

Use the pants pattern given on page 11, cutting the legs so that they will reach to just below knee length on the child. Make the pants following the instructions given with the pants pattern, then try them on the child with the wrong side outside. Pin a dart in each side of the pants to make them fit closely to the legs, taking care to leave them loose enough to be taken off. Sew the darts as pinned and then trim off the excess fabric. Hem the lower leg edges and turn the pants right side out. Sew three buttons to each side of the pants at the knee.

Neck Scarf

Use a man's handkerchief.

Apron

46 cm ($\frac{1}{2}$ yd) of 92 cm (36 in.) wide cotton fabric will make the apron. Cut a 46 cm by 56 cm (18 in. by 22 in.) piece off the fabric and use the remainder for the waistband. Pleat one 56 cm (22 in.) edge to measure 35.5 cm (14 in.) then hem the remaining raw edges. Sew the pleated edge to the waistband.

Tray of hot cross buns

Materials

Old nylon tights or stockings.
Brown and pale yellow felt.
A reddish brown pencil.
Cotton wool or kapok for stuffing the buns.
A cardboard grocery carton cut down to measure about 23 cm by 30.5 cm by 4 cm (9 in. by 12 in. by 1$\frac{1}{2}$ in.) deep, for the tray.
Piece of white fabric for the tray-cloth.
4 cm (1$\frac{1}{2}$ in.) wide fawn coloured furnishing braid long enough to go round the sides of the tray.
A boot lace or length of cord for the neck strap.
White card and two needles for the price tickets.
Adhesive.

To make the tray

Glue the ends of the boot lace or cord to the sides of the tray and underneath, leaving the strap long enough so that the tray will be about waist height when worn. Glue the furnishing braid around the sides of the tray. Place the piece of fabric for the tray-cloth in the tray and glue it down here and there to hold it in position.

To make the price tickets

Cut four price tickets from white card to the shape shown in the illustration. Glue them together in pairs, sandwiching the blunt end of a needle between each pair. Mark the words on each ticket.

To make the buns

For the 'one-a-penny' buns, cut a 13 cm (5 in.) diameter circle of nylon stocking fabric and a 10 cm (4 in.) diameter circle of brown felt. Run a gathering thread round the edge of the nylon circle then place the felt circle inside the nylon circle and stuff it firmly, pulling the gathering thread up tight to stretch the nylon fabric. The bun should measure about 9 cm (3½ in.) across. Fasten off the gathering thread.

Moisten the reddish brown pencil and rub it on top of the bun then rub the colour into the fabric with the fingertips. For the pastry crosses cut strips

of yellow felt roughly 1.3 cm (½ in.) wide by 5.5 cm (2¼ in.) long. Colour the edges of these felt strips with brown pencil before gluing them to the top of the bun.

Make the 'two-a-penny' buns in the same way using a 9 cm (3½ in.) diameter circle of nylon fabric, a 7 cm (2¾ in.) diameter circle of felt and 4.5 cm (1¾ in.) long strips for the pastry crosses. Glue the buns to the tray if desired.

41

Ancient Egyptian Costume

White butter muslin is used double for the dress and cape illustrated, but any kind of fine cotton fabric in pastel colours would be suitable. The collar and bracelets are made by sticking a variety of gold, red and blue braids and cords on to firm interlining shapes. Ring-pulls, saved from the tops of drinks cans and painted gold, also make a very effective decoration on the collar. Alternatively, beads, buttons, curtain rings, paper clips etc., can be used.

If the child has naturally dark hair, the wig can be omitted and only the headband needs to be made.

Dress and shoulder cape

Materials required for height 142 cm (4 ft 8 in.)

5.8 m (6¼ yd) of 92 cm (36 in.) wide butter muslin; note that only half this yardage is required if thicker cotton fabric is used.
70 cm (¾ yd) of narrow elastic.
One hook and eye.
70 cm (¾ yd) of narrow tape for the dress shoulder straps.

To make the dress

Cut two pieces of muslin 92 cm (36 in.) wide by twice the child's underarm to ankle measurement. Join these two pieces at the long edges forming a long tube of fabric. Hem the remaining raw edges at each end of the tube. Fold the tube in half, back on itself, to form a double thickness tube, having the right side of the fabric outside. Hem the top folded edge of the tube to form a casing for the elastic, then thread elastic through to fit the child's chest.

Put the dress on the child and attach lengths of tape to the top of the dress to go over each shoulder to hold the dress up.

To make the cape

Make a pattern for the cape by drawing out a 71 cm (28 in.) diameter circle with a 13 cm (5 in.) diameter circle cut out of the centre. Cut the cape from double thickness muslin then make a cut from the outer to the inner edge as shown in diagram 1.

Join the two cape pieces round the inner and outer curved edges leaving the straight front edges open. Turn right side out and press. Turn in the

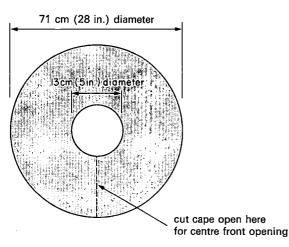

71 cm (28 in.) diameter

l3cm (5in.) diameter

cut cape open here
for centre front opening

1. *The cape pattern.*

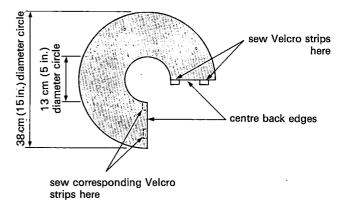

38cm (15 in.) diameter circle

13 cm (5 in.) diameter circle

sew Velcro strips here

centre back edges

sew corresponding Velcro
strips here

2. *The collar pattern.*

front edges and run a gathering thread along each one, pull up the gathers tightly and fasten off the threads. Sew a hook and eye to the gathered edges.

Girdle

For this use 2 to 3 m (yd) of silky gold coloured cord. Knot and fringe out the ends of the cord, then tie the girdle round the waist as illustrated.

Collar

Materials required to fit any size

92 cm (1 yd) of 82 cm (32 in.) wide firm interlining. Oddment of gold coloured fabric at least 40.5 cm (16 in.) square for covering the collar shape.
5 cm (2 in.) strip of Velcro.
Ric-rac braids, cords, tapes, coloured paper or cord or any suitable materials for trimming the collar.
Adhesive.

To make

Cut two 38 cm (15 in.) diameter circles of interlining then cut 13 cm (5 in.) diameter circles from the centres and discard them. Glue the two pieces together. Cut away one quarter of the remaining shape to give the collar shape shown in diagram 2.

Spread adhesive all round the edges of the shape and stick it on the piece of gold fabric. Cut out the fabric allowing 1.3 cm ($\frac{1}{2}$ in.) extra all round the collar shape. Turn the 1.3 cm ($\frac{1}{2}$ in.) extra on to the other side of the collar and stick it in place. Sew on two 2.5 cm (1 in.) strips of Velcro at the positions indicated in diagram 2.

Now glue trimmings etc. to the collar. The ring-pulls in the collar illustrated have circles of red paper glued in the rings and, in between them, triangles of blue paper. Metal pieces may require a preliminary coat of glue which should be left to dry before finally sticking the pieces to the collar.

44

Bracelets

Materials required to fit any size

Small pieces of firm interlining and gold coloured fabric.
Two 5 cm (2 in.) strips of Velcro.
Braids and cords as for the collar.
Adhesive.

To make

For each one, cut two 6.5 cm (2½ in.) wide strips of interlining by the child's wrist measurement plus 1.3 cm (½ in.). Glue the strips together in pairs. Cover the pieces with fabric and glue on trimmings in the same way as given for the collar. Sew a strip of Velcro to each bracelet at the short edges.

Sandals

The feet can be bare but sandals are easy to make using as a basis plastic flip-flop sandals.

First remove the plastic toe straps on the sandals and replace these with strips of narrow braid going from the toe hole to the arch of the foot. Another strip of braid goes across the foot and then the first strip is joined on to it as shown in diagram 3. Knot the ends of the braid tightly underneath the soles, the knots will sink in to the recesses there. Glue strips of braid round the edge of the soles. Make a small ornamental piece for each sandal in the same way as for the collar using small strips of interlining as foundations. Glue the ornamental pieces in place on the straps as shown in diagram 3.

The wig

Materials required to fit any size

Two 50 gram balls of black chunky knitting yarn.
A circle of black fabric about 30.5 cm (12 in.) in diameter.
Two 2.5 cm (1 in.) wide strips of firm interlining

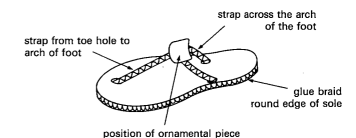

strap from toe hole to arch of foot

strap across the arch of the foot

glue braid round edge of sole

position of ornamental piece

3. *Making the sandals.*

long enough to go round the child's head plus 2.5 cm (1 in.), for the headband.
Gold fabric for covering the headband.
1.4 m (1½ yd) of gold ric-rac braid.
Adhesive.

To make

For the headband glue the strips of interlining together and cover with fabric in the same way as given for the collar.

For the lengths of hair which hang down all round, make a template of cardboard measuring 25.5 cm by 15 cm (10 in. by 6 in.). Cut a 3 m (3 yd) length of yarn and wind it round and round the card as shown in diagram 4, holding the ends in

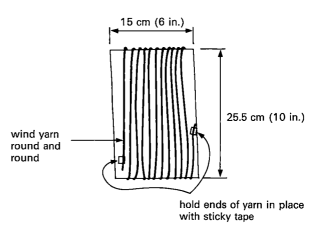

15 cm (6 in.)

25.5 cm (10 in.)

wind yarn round and round

hold ends of yarn in place with sticky tape

4. *Winding the yarn round the piece of card.*

45

5. *Sewing the yarn strands to the headband.*

leave a gap of 13 cm (5 in.) at centre for face

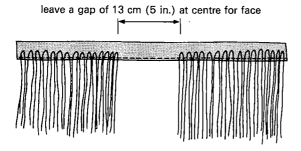

6. *Stitching the yarn strands to the oval of fabric.*

finally stitch yarn strands to fabric
1.3 cm (½ in.) from edge all around

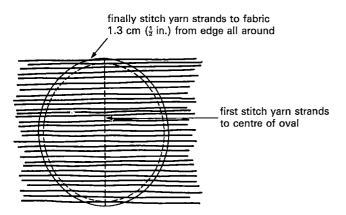

first stitch yarn strands
to centre of oval

place with bits of sticky tape. Now *very carefully* steam this yarn using either a steam iron or steam from a kettle spout. This will make the yarn strands quite straight but take care not to get burned.

Cut through the yarn strands at one end of the card and carefully take the folded ends and stitch them to the inside of the headband as shown in diagram 5. Continue making yarn strands and sewing them to the headband in this way until it is completed, leaving a gap of about 13 cm (5 in.) at the centre of the band for the face.

Now place the band around the child's head, overlap the back edges as necessary to fit, then stitch them together. Glue two rows of gold ric-rac to the band.

For the top part of the wig, place the 30.5 cm (12 in.) diameter circle of black fabric on top of the child's head and then put the headband in position over it. Mark the position of the top edge of the headband on to the fabric circle all round. Remove the fabric and cut it out 1.3 cm (½ in.) larger all round than the marked shape. The final shape will be slightly oval.

To cover this oval shape with yarn, wind strands of the remaining yarn around the card, steam, then cut through the yarn strands at both ends. Stitch the yarn strands to the centre of the

ease into small pleats
at intervals all
round to fit

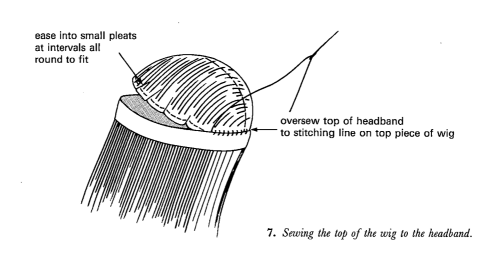

oversew top of headband
to stitching line on top piece of wig

7. *Sewing the top of the wig to the headband.*

oval of fabric as shown in diagram 6. Continue until the fabric is completely covered. Now stitch the yarn strands to the fabric all round 1.3 cm ($\frac{1}{2}$ in.) from the edge as shown in diagram 6. Cut the yarn strands level with the fabric shape all round.

Lap the top of the headband 1.3 cm ($\frac{1}{2}$ in.) over the raw edge of the oval shape and slip stitch it in place as shown in diagram 7 easing the fabric in to small pleats at intervals to make it fit. Note that the stitching for the centre 'parting' of the wig should be in line with the centre front of the headband.

Finally, steam the lengths of yarn once more and cut the ends to an even length all round.

If the child has long hair, gather it to the nape of the neck and pin in a flat bun so that it is hidden by the wig.

Make-up

Use face cream and talcum powder to whiten the face then colour the cheeks and mouth with orange lipstick. Colour the area above the eyes with green eye shadow, then outline the eyes and eyebrows with black, extending the lines outward at the outer corners of the eye.

Queen of Hearts

The Queen wears an outfit in playing card colours of royal blue, red, yellow, white and black. A red T-shirt is used as a basis for the top of the costume; black, white and blue are also suitable colours. The heart-shaped tarts are made of yellow felt, red cellophane and foil sweet wrappings.

Skirt, top, collar and crown

Materials required for height 142 cm (4 ft 8 in.)

A red, white, black or blue T-shirt, either sleeveless or with short sleeves.

1.9 m (2 yd) of 122 cm (48 in.) wide royal blue curtain fabric.

92 cm (1 yd) of 122 cm (48 in.) wide yellow curtain fabric.

46 cm ($\frac{1}{2}$ yd) of 92 cm (36 in.) wide white curtain net for the collar frill and the chin veil on the crown.

5.5 m (6 yd) of black bias binding.

2.8 m (3 yd) of yellow bias binding.

92 cm (1 yd) of red bias binding.

A length of 2.5 cm (1 in.) wide black petersham ribbon the child's waist measurement plus 8 cm (3 in.), for the skirt waistband.

15 cm (6 in.) strip of Velcro for skirt and back collar fastenings, or hooks and eyes instead. Two strips of white fleecy fabric or felt measuring 6.5 cm by 61 cm ($2\frac{1}{2}$ in. by 24 in.).

Piece of red felt for the heart shapes, measuring 18 cm by 61 cm (7 in. by 24 in.).

92 cm (1 yd) of 82 cm (32 in.) wide firm interlining for hat, collar and bodice front.

Adhesive.

To make the skirt

Cut a 1.9 m (2 yd) long strip of royal blue fabric making the width the measurement from the child's waist to floor level as shown in diagram 1. The remaining piece of fabric is for the sleeves. Cut out the four sleeve pieces as shown in diagram 1.

From the yellow fabric cut the strip which will be sewn to the centre front of the skirt. This should measure 9 cm ($3\frac{1}{2}$ in.) in width at the waist edge, broadening out to 35.5 cm (14 in.) at the hem, and the same length exactly as for the skirt length. Glue the raw edges of this piece to the skirt, then sew on black bias binding to cover the long raw edges of the yellow strip.

From red felt cut out the largest heart shape to the size shown in diagram 2, then cut out four more hearts making each one about 0.6 cm ($\frac{1}{4}$ in.) smaller all round than the one before. Glue or sew the hearts in place on the yellow skirt strip as illustrated.

Join the short edges of the skirt for the centre back seam from the hem edge to within 15 cm (6 in.) of the waist edge, taking a 2.5 cm (1 in.) seam. Press the seam to one side. The opening at the top forms the skirt opening. Gather the waist edge of the skirt to fit the child's waist, sew it to the length of ribbon then sew Velcro or hooks and eyes at the waistband overlap. Hem the lower edge of the skirt.

To make the dress top

Join the sleeve pieces in pairs along the 46 cm (18 in.) edges. These form the overarm seams. Join the tapered edges for the underarm seams. Turn in the narrow ends which are the armhole edges of the sleeves, and tack or stitch these to the armholes of the T-shirt. If the T-shirt has short sleeves these will be inside the blue fabric sleeves. Try the dress top on the child to see if the wrist edges of the sleeves need to be shortened and cut off any excess.

Turn the wrist edges of the sleeves 0.6 cm ($\frac{1}{4}$ in.) to the outside and press.

Bind the long edges of the strips of white fleecy fabric or felt with yellow bias binding, then sew each one round the wrist edge of each sleeve to cover the raw edges.

Cut sixteen red felt hearts to the size shown in diagram 3 and glue eight to each white fleecy strip as illustrated.

From the yellow fabric, cut the strip which will be sewn to the centre front of the T-shirt. This should measure 15 cm (6 in.) at the top edge

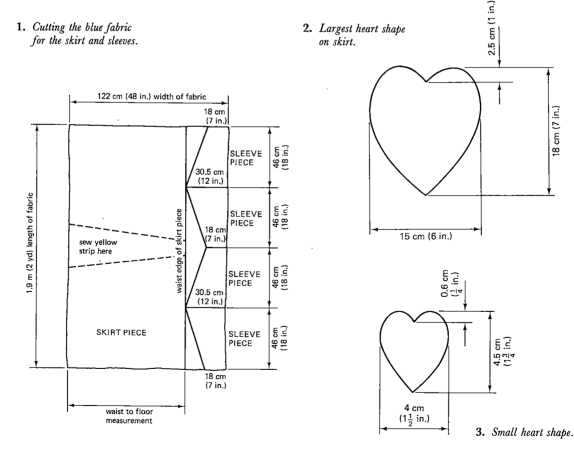

1. *Cutting the blue fabric for the skirt and sleeves.*

2. *Largest heart shape on skirt.*

3. *Small heart shape.*

tapering to 9 cm (3½ in.) at the lower edge by 35.5 cm (14 in.) in length. Cut two pieces of interlining the same size and glue them to the wrong side of the yellow strip. Bind the long raw edges of the strip with black bias binding and tack or stitch it round the edges to the centre front of the T-shirt.

To make the collar

Cut a 40.5 cm (16 in.) diameter circle of interlining with a 13 cm (5 in.) diameter hole cut out of the centre for the neck edge. Cut away one quarter of the circle and discard it. Cut another piece in the same way, then glue the pieces together. Glue the interlining collar shape on to the wrong side of a piece of yellow fabric then cut out the fabric level with the interlining. Cover the other side of the interlining in the same way.

Sew a strip of black bias binding round the collar about 4 cm (1½ in.) from the outer edge, then bind the outer edge and the short straight edges with black bias.

For the collar frill, cut a 20.5 by 86.5 cm (8 in. by 34 in.) strip of white net fabric, fold in half widthways and gather up the long edges to fit the neck edge of the collar. Stitch the gathered edge of the frill in place. Bind the neck edge of the collar with red bias, then sew an 8 cm (3 in.) strip of Velcro or hooks and eyes to the short straight edges for the back collar fastening.

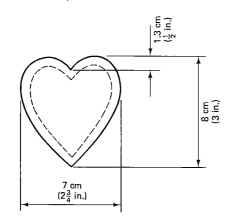

4. *Heart shape for the tarts.*

To make the crown

Cut two 13 cm (5 in.) wide strips of interlining to fit around the child's head plus 0.6 cm (¼ in.) for the overlap. Glue them together. Cover both sides of the interlining with yellow fabric in the same way as for the collar. Fold the strip into four along the length, then along one side cut out a curve through all thicknesses using the edge of a saucer as a guide. This will give the crown four points when the strip is opened up. Bind the upper curved edges with black bias and the lower edge with red bias. Overlap the short edges 0.6 cm (¼ in.) and glue or stitch in place. Cut out four red felt hearts to the size shown in diagram 3 and glue them to the crown as illustrated.

For the chin veil, cut an 18 cm by 40.5 cm (7 in. by 16 in.) strip of white net fabric and hem the edges. Gather up the short edges and sew one to each side of the crown to pass under the chin.

Hip pad

To make the skirt stand out around the hips make a hip pad from a nylon stocking stuffed into a sausage shape about 56 cm (22 in.) in length. Gather each end and sew on a length of tape so that the pad can be tied on just below the child's waist.

Plate of tarts

Materials

A piece of yellow or fawn felt for the pastry.
Red cellophane and foil sweet wrappings for the jam.
A paper plate or small baking tray.
Brown and red felt-tipped pens.
Adhesive.

To make

For one tart, cut out two heart shapes from felt to the sizes shown in diagram 4. Cut the centre out of one heart shape and discard it, leaving about 0.6 cm ($\frac{1}{4}$ in.) round the edges as shown by the dotted line on the diagram.

Cut heart shapes from foil and cellophane making them slightly smaller all round. Glue the foil to the felt heart, the cellophane to the foil and finally glue the felt heart with the cut out centre on top.

Colour the outer edges of the felt with brown pen and the inner edges with red. Make as many tarts as desired and glue them to the plate or tray.

Knave of Hearts

The Knave wears a costume to match the Queen's. A long sleeved T-shirt, shirt or sweater, and tights are used as a basis for the outfit. These can be in any of the playing card colours of royal blue, red, yellow, white or black.

Sweater and tights

Any of the colours listed above are suitable.

Shoes

Use black gym shoes. Cut two heart shapes from red felt about the size of the tarts given in diagram 4 in the Queen of Hearts instructions. Glue or pin the hearts to the fronts of the shoes as illustrated.

Tunic, collar, cuffs and crown

Materials required for height 142 cm (4 ft 8 in.)

1.4 m (1½ yd) of 122 cm (48 in.) wide royal blue curtain fabric.
92 cm (1 yd) of 122 cm (48 in.) wide yellow curtain fabric.
92 cm (¹ yd) of ready frilled lace edging for the collar and cuff frills.
4.4 m (4¾ yd) of black bias binding.

1.2 m (1¼ yd) of broad black ric-rac braid for trimming the collar.
1.9 m (2 yd) of yellow bias binding.
92 cm (1 yd) of red bias binding.
13 cm (5 in.) strip of Velcro for back collar fastening or hooks and eyes instead.
Two strips of white fleecy fabric or felt measuring 6.5 cm by 46 cm (2½ in. by 18 in.).
Piece of red felt for the heart shapes measuring 25.5 cm by 46 cm (10 in. by 18 in.).
140 cm (1½ yd) of 82 cm (32 in.) wide firm interlining for collar, cuffs and crown.
Adhesive.

To make the tunic

Use the tunic pattern given on page 9, shortening the sleeve edges to the lines marked B. Place the pattern against the child to check that the hem edge comes slightly lower than the tops of the legs and shorten or lengthen the pattern as necessary.

Cut the tunic from royal blue fabric, then cut out the V-neckline on the front of the tunic only. For the yellow panel down the front of the tunic cut a strip of yellow fabric measuring 15 cm (6 in.) across at the neck edge and broadening out to 30.5 cm (12 in.) at the hem edge of the tunic. Glue the raw edges of this piece to the centre front of the tunic, then sew on black bias binding to cover the long raw edges of the yellow strip. Bind the neck edge with black bias binding.

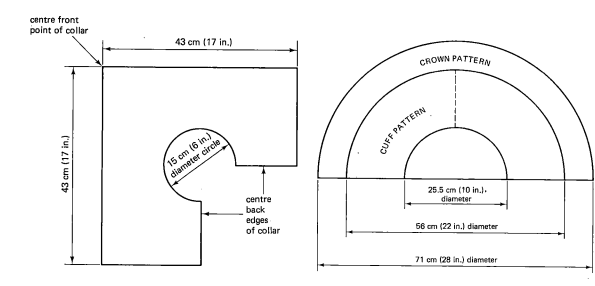

centre front
point of collar

43 cm (17 in.)

43 cm (17 in.)

15 cm (6 in.) diameter circle

centre
back
edges
of collar

CROWN PATTERN

CUFF PATTERN

25.5 cm (10 in.), diameter

56 cm (22 in.) diameter

71 cm (28 in.) diameter

1. *The collar shape.*

2. *The crown and cuff pattern shapes.*

From red felt cut out the largest heart shape as given in diagram 2 in the Queen of Hearts instructions, then cut out another heart about 0.6 cm (¼ in.) smaller all round. Glue or sew the hearts to the yellow strip as illustrated.

Join the side and underarm seams of the tunic and clip the underarm curves. Try the tunic on the child to see if larger turnings need to be taken on these seams to make the tunic fit neatly. Hem the sleeve and lower edges.

To make the collar

Cut a 43 cm (17 in.) square of firm interlining. Cut away one quarter of this square and discard it. Draw and cut out a 15 cm (6 in.) diameter circle at the centre of the square as shown in diagram 1. This forms the collar shape. Try the collar shape on the child, bringing the centre back edges together, then trim a little off the outer edges if the collar looks too large for the child. Cut another piece in the same way then glue the pieces together.

Spread glue on the edges of one side of the collar and place it on a piece of the yellow fabric, then cut out the fabric level with the collar shape. Repeat this on the other side of the interlining. Bind the neck edge of the collar with red bias binding and the remaining raw edges with black bias binding. Sew on the ric-rac braid as illustrated. Glue or sew on a heart shape cut from red felt, making it about 0.6 cm (¼ in.) smaller all round than the smallest heart on the tunic. Sew frilled edging to the neck edge of the collar and then sew Velcro or hooks and eyes to the centre back edges.

To make the cuffs and crown

Make a paper pattern for these by drawing and cutting out a 71 cm (28 in.) diameter semi-circle. Draw another two semi-circles within the first, making one 56 cm (22 in.) diameter and one 25.5 cm (10 in.) diameter as shown in diagram 2. Cut out the 25.5 cm (10 in.) diameter semi-circle and discard it. Cut out the 56 cm (22 in.) diameter semi-circle and cut it in half on the dotted line

56

indicated in the diagram; use only one of these pieces for the cuff pattern. The remaining narrow piece is the crown pattern. Place it on the child's head, overlapping and cutting the short edges to make it fit, leaving 0.6 cm ($\frac{1}{4}$ in.) extra for an overlap.

Cut two cuff pieces from interlining for each cuff and glue them together, then cover both sides of each piece with royal blue fabric in the same way as for the collar. Overlap the straight edges of each cuff 0.6 cm ($\frac{1}{4}$ in.) and glue, then try the cuffs on the child to see that they will slide over the hands easily. If the narrow end is too tight trim a little off it. If the cuffs are too long for the child, trim the other ends to size. Sew frilled edging to the narrow wrist edges of the cuffs.

Bind one long edge of each strip of white fleecy fabric or felt with yellow bias binding, stretching the binding as it is sewn on to draw up the edge of the white fabric and make it shorter. Join the short edges of each white strip. Tack the remaining raw edges of the white strips to the wide edges of the cuffs with the raw edges even. Bind these edges with yellow bias binding.

For each cuff cut out six small red felt heart shapes as given in diagram 3 in the Queen of Hearts' instructions. Glue them to the white fabric at even intervals as shown in the illustration.

Cut two crown shapes from interlining and glue them together then cover both sides with yellow fabric in the same way as given for the collar. Overlap the short edges of the crown 0.6 cm ($\frac{1}{4}$ in.) and glue. Bind the upper edge with black bias binding and the lower edge with red. Cut out four red felt heart shapes and glue them to the crown at intervals as illustrated.

Plate of tarts

Make in the same way as given for the Queen of Hearts.

Frog Prince and Princess

The frog is in fact a little floppy 'bean' bag made from velvet and filled with either rice or lentils.

Materials

Two 20.5 cm (8 in.) squares of green velvet or felt, if possible having one square a shade lighter than the other.
140 g (5 oz) of rice or lentils.
Two 1.3 cm ($\frac{1}{2}$ in.) diameter black or brown beads for eyes.
Scrap of orange felt.
Black permanent marker pen.
Adhesive.

To make

The frog patterns (diagram 1) are given here actual size. Trace them off the page using thin paper then cut out the paper patterns. Place the two squares of velvet or felt right sides together and pin the body pattern on to this double thickness. Machine stitch all round the paper shape, exactly at the edges, leaving a gap in the seam as indicated on the pattern. Remove the paper pattern, then cut out the frog about 0.3 cm ($\frac{1}{8}$ in.) from the line of stitching. Turn right side out.

Fill the frog with the rice or lentils using a little funnel shape made from paper to do this more easily. Turn in the remaining raw edges and slip stitch the gap. Mark the darker side of the frog with spots and blotches as illustrated using black pen.

Cut 0.3 cm ($\frac{1}{8}$ in.) wide strips of orange felt and glue around each bead making the hole in the bead the centre of the eye as shown in diagram 2. Cut a 5 cm (2 in.) square of the darker green velvet or felt from the pieces left over after cutting out the frog. Spread glue on the wrong side of the square and fold it in half with the glued sides together. From this piece, cut out two eyelids placing the eyelid pattern against the fold in the fabric as shown on the pattern. Glue an eyelid over each eye, then glue the eyes in place as shown on the pattern.

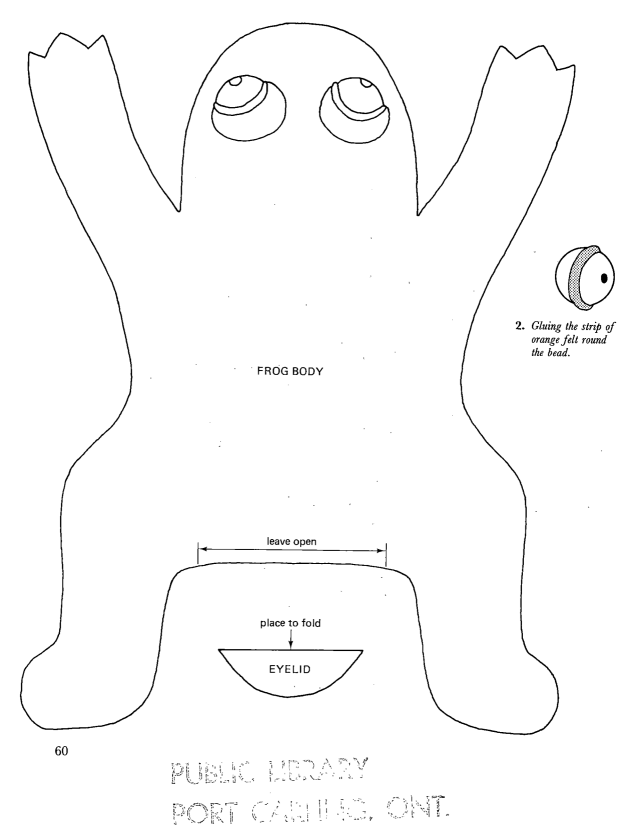

FROG BODY

2. *Gluing the strip of orange felt round the bead.*

leave open

place to fold

EYELID

The princess outfit is very quick and easy to make.

The princess's dress and headband

Materials required for height 142 cm (4 ft 8 in.)

2.8 cm (3 yd) of 122 cm (48 in.) wide brocade curtain fabric.
5.5 m (6 yd) of braid for edging the dress and the undersleeves and for the headband.
23 cm (¼ yd) of 122 cm (48 in.) wide curtain velvet for the undersleeves and neck trimming.
46 cm (½ yd) of narrow elastic.
2.8 m (3 yd) of thick silky dressing gown cord for the girdle.
A chiffon scarf or piece of thin fabric for the veil.

To make

Use the tunic pattern given on page 9 as a basis for cutting out the dress as shown in diagram 3. Cut the sleeve edges to the full width of the fabric taking the underarm sleeve edges almost to the full length of the fabric. Cut the lower edge to the required length to make the dress floor level on the child. Cut out the V-neckline on the front and the back of the dress.

Join the entire side and underarm sleeve seams of the dress and clip the underarm curves. Try the dress on the child to see if larger underarm seams need to be taken; this will probably be necessary to give a neater armhole fit.

Now join the sleeve edges from the pointed end to within 38 cm (15 in.) of the upper folded edge. Turn the dress right side out, then turn in and hem the remaining raw edges of the sleeves.

Cut the front V-neckline a little lower than the back, then turn in the neck edge 0.6 cm (¼ in.) and stitch, clipping the edge if necessary to make it turn. Hem the lower edge of the dress.

Stitch braid trimming to the neck, sleeve and lower edges. Run a gathering thread along the top folded edge of each sleeve from the braid trimming for 20.5 cm (8 in.) as shown in diagram 3, pull up

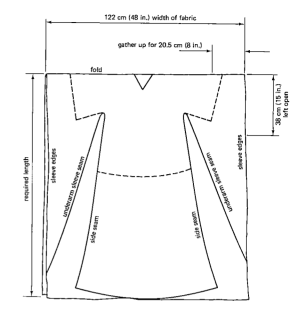

3. *Cutting out the dress and sleeves, (dotted lines show the original tunic pattern size).*

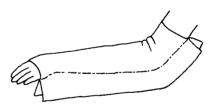

4. *Pinning the sleeve fabric around the hand and arm.*

the gathers tightly and fasten off the threads.

For each undersleeve cut a 23 cm by 40.5 cm (9 in. by 16 in.) strip of velvet. With the right side inside, pin the strips around the child's arms as shown in diagram 4, with the 40.5 cm (16 in.)

length along the length of the arms. The fabric should come well down over the hands and the sleeves should be pinned loosely enough to be taken off and on. Take off the sleeves and sew the seams as pinned. Trim off the excess fabric at the seams and then hem the upper and lower edges. Trim the lower edges with braid and thread elastic through the upper edges to fit the child's arms.

For the velvet piece at the front neck edge of the dress, cut a triangle of velvet to fit, hem and trim the upper edge with braid, then sew the triangle in position on the inside of the dress.

For the headband, cut a length of braid to go around the child's head plus a little extra for a seam. Sew the ends of the braid together, then sew the scarf or fabric to the headband to hang down the back as illustrated.

For the girdle, tie a knot in each end of the cord and tie it around the dress as illustrated.

The golden ball

Use a shiny golden Christmas tree decoration.

1920s evening dress

This outfit is quick and easy to make using satin dress lining fabric for the basic dress and curtain net in the same colour for the 'handkerchief panels' skirt. The dress illustrated is in vivid orange but any bright colour is suitable. Sequin and bead trimmings were very popular at this period and these can be applied as lavishly as desired.

Dress and headband

Materials required for height 142 cm (4 ft 8 in.)

1.4 m (1½ yd) of 92 cm (36 in.) wide satin dress lining fabric.
2.8 m (3 yd) of 122 cm (48 in.) wide curtain net in the same colour as the satin fabric.
2.1 m (2¼ yd) of silver sequins.
2.1 m (2¼ yd) of contrasting coloured sequins.
Snap fasteners for the dress back fastening and the headband.
Feather for trimming the headband if available.

To make the dress

For the dress bodice cut a rectangle of satin fabric to the measurements shown in diagram 1. Fold this bodice piece in half with the right side of the fabric outside, along the line indicated and press. The folded edge is the top edge of the bodice. Turn

in the centre back raw edges 2.5 cm (1 in.) and stitch in place. Sew a row of each colour of sequins round the top of the bodice as shown in the illustration.

For the bodice straps, cut a 6.5 cm (2½ in.) wide strip of satin fabric 61 cm (24 in.) in length. Turn in each of the long raw edges of the strip 2 cm (¾ in.) and press, making a 2.5 cm (1 in.) wide strip. Stitch down the centre of the strip to hold the raw edges in place. Cut the strip in two pieces. Place the dress bodice around the child and overlap and pin the back edges as necessary to make it fit. Pin the straps in position on the front and back of the bodice, shortening them as necessary to make the bodice fit neatly underneath the arms. Mark the position of the ends of the straps on the bodice with pins. Sew two rows of sequins to each strap then sew the ends of the straps in position on the inside of the bodice.

For the dress skirt, cut a 92 cm (36 in.) wide strip of satin fabric long enough to reach from the lower edge of the dress bodice to above the child's knees. Note that for a very small child the 92 cm (36 in.) width may give too much fullness in the skirt, so instead, make the skirt the child's hip measurement plus 15 cm (6 in.). Join the short edges of the skirt strip leaving about 10 cm (4 in.) open at the top of the seam for the back skirt opening. Press the seam to one side. Slightly gather the upper edge of the skirt until it fits the lower edge of the bodice,

1. *How to cut the dress bodice piece.*

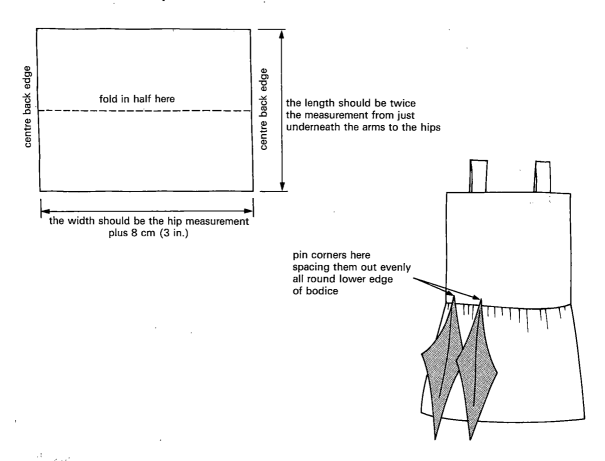

centre back edge

fold in half here

centre back edge

the length should be twice
the measurement from just
underneath the arms to the hips

the width should be the hip measurement
plus 8 cm (3 in.)

pin corners here
spacing them out evenly
all round lower edge
of bodice

2. *Pinning the first lot of handkerchief panels in place.*

For the band around the hips cut a 10 cm (4 in.) wide strip of net fabric long enough to go around the lower edge of the dress bodice. Join the long edges taking a 0.6 cm ($\frac{1}{4}$ in.) seam. Turn the strip right side out and press. Sew one long edge of the strip in position at the lower edge of the bodice covering the top points of the handkerchief squares. Sew the short edges of the strip to the centre back edges of the bodice.

Make a bow from a scrap of the net fabric and sew it to the band at one side of the dress. Sew snap fasteners to the centre back overlap.

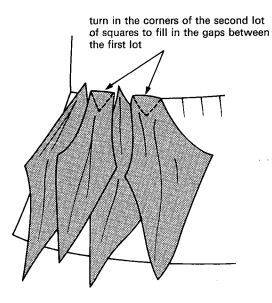

turn in the corners of the second lot of squares to fill in the gaps between the first lot

3. *Pinning the second lot of handkerchief panels in place.*

To make the headband

Using satin lining fabric, make a strip in the same way as given for the bodice straps. Cut the strip to fit around the child's head leaving 4 cm (1½ in.) extra for neatening the ends and an overlap. Neaten the ends, then sew two rows of sequins to the strip as shown in the illustration. Sew snap fasteners to the overlap.

Make a small bow from a scrap of net fabric and sew it to one side of the headband along with the feather.

Shoes

If possible, the shoes should have little heels and straps going across the instep. Alternatively, plain, flat slippers can be used with a band of ribbon sewn across the instep.

Jewellery

Long strings of beads, especially pearls, dangling ear-rings, and slave bangles are all suitable.

Hairstyle

Short hair is the correct style for this period, but long hair can be swept up at the back and pinned as flat as possible. The headband will help to hold it in place.

Make-up

Colour the cheeks and lips with red lipstick. Eyebrows can also be pencilled in, making a thin line.

Tudor Costume c.1530

This type of costume with the gable head-dress and huge cuffs was worn during the reign of Henry VIII. Green velvet curtain fabric is used for the dress illustrated here but plain non-woven curtain fabric would also be suitable. Other colours fashionable at the time were shades of red, orange, blue and grey. If desired, plain brocade material can be used for the turned-back cuffs instead of fur fabric.

Dress

Materials required for height 142 cm (4 ft 8 in.)

3 m (3¼ yd) of 122 cm (48 in.) wide velvet or other plain curtain fabric.

46 cm (½ yd) of 122 cm (48 in.) wide patterned brocade curtain fabric for the under sleeves.

92 cm (1 yd) of 122 cm (48 in.) wide fur fabric or brocade curtain fabric for the turned-back sleeve cuffs.

Strip of cotton fabric for lining the bodice the same size as given for the bodice in the making-up instructions.

2.3 m (2½ yd) of 2.5 cm (1 in.) wide lace edging for trimming the under sleeves and the bodice neckline.

1.4 m (1½ yd) each of 2 cm (¾ in.) wide braid and very narrow braid for trimming the bodice neckline.

Hooks and eyes for the back bodice fastening. 46 cm (½ yd) narrow elastic.

To make the skirt

Make a quarter circle paper pattern for the skirt drawing it to the sizes given in diagram 1. Place the edge of the pattern marked 'fold' against a fold in the velvet fabric, then cut out the skirt from the double thickness of fabric to give the full size semicircular shaped skirt.

Join the straight edges of the semicircle taking a 2.5 cm (1 in.) seam and leaving 15 cm (6 in.) open

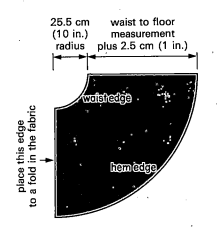

25.5 cm (10 in.) radius — waist to floor measurement plus 2.5 cm (1 in.)

place this edge to a fold in the fabric

waist edge

hem edge

1. *The skirt pattern.*

68

at the waist edge of the seam for the centre back skirt opening. Press the seam to one side. Do not hem the lower edge of the skirt at this stage.

To make the bodice

Cut a strip of velvet fabric to the measurements given in diagram 2. Cut a strip of lining fabric the same size. Join the lining to the bodice strip as shown in diagram 2 leaving the waist edges open. Turn the bodice right side out and press. Tack the waist edges together.

For the shoulder straps cut a 5 cm by 61 cm (2 in. by 24 in.) strip of velvet fabric. Join the long raw edges of the strip, turn it right side out and press. Cut the strip into two pieces.

Place the bodice inside out around the child's chest overlapping and pinning the short edges at the centre back to fit. Pin the ends of the shoulder straps to the bodice as shown in diagram 3, shortening the straps as necessary to make the bodice fit neatly under the arms. Pin a dart in each side of the bodice through both thicknesses of fabric from the waist edge tapering to the top edge as shown in diagram 3, to make the bodice fit neatly round the waist.

Take off the bodice, stitch the darts as pinned then sew the ends of the straps in place. Sew one edge of the lace edging to the inside of the neck edge and straps as shown in the illustration.

For the sleeves, make a pattern as shown in diagram 4. First of all draw out a 20.5 cm (8 in.) diameter semicircle then extend the straight edge and add a piece to each side as shown by the dotted lines on the diagram. Finally curve the sharp corners at the top part of the sleeves.

Cut two sleeves from velvet and join the underarm edges of each one. Pin the curved top edge of each sleeve 1.3 cm ($\frac{1}{2}$ in.) under each shoulder strap then pin the remainder of the top sleeve edge to the inside of the bodice at the underarm. Note that for smaller sizes, the sleeves may have to be cut a little smaller all round to fit the armhole size of the bodice. Sew the sleeves in place as pinned. Stitch the braids to the neck edge

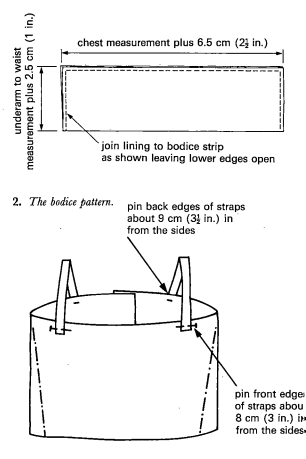

2. *The bodice pattern.*

pin back edges of straps about 9 cm (3½ in.) in from the sides

pin front edges of straps about 8 cm (3 in.) in from the sides

3. *Pinning on the shoulder straps and side darts.*

of the bodice and straps as illustrated.

Gather the waist edge of the skirt to fit the lower edge of the bodice. Sew the waist edge of the skirt to the lower edge of the bodice. Try the dress on the child and turn up the lower edge to make the skirt floor length. Hem the lower edge. Sew hooks and eyes to the back edges of the dress.

To make the brocade undersleeves

Cut two 46 cm by 51 cm (18 in. by 20 in.) pieces of fabric. Join the 46 cm (18 in.) edges of each piece.

Hem one remaining raw edge on each sleeve and stitch lace edging to it for the cuff frill. Thread elastic through the hemmed edges to fit the child's wrists.

Put the dress on the child and then try on the brocade sleeves. The upper raw edges should extend about 15 cm (6 in.) above the elbows. If the brocade sleeves are too long cut the upper raw edges to fit. Turn in the upper raw edges and gather them to fit the lower edges of the velvet dress sleeves. Lap the gathered edges 1.3 cm (½ in.) over the velvet sleeve edges and slip stitch in place.

To make the turned-back cuffs

Cut two 40.5 cm by 102 cm (16 in. by 40 in.) strips of fur fabric or brocade. Note that for smaller sizes, these cuffs should be made proportionately smaller. The illustration gives a guide as to the correct length of the cuffs in relation to the costume.

Fold the cuff pieces in half bringing the 40.5 cm (16 in.) edges together then stitch the seam as shown in diagram 5. Trim off the excess pieces as indicated in the diagram. If the cuffs are made from brocade, hem the remaining raw edges. Fur fabric edges do not require hemming.

Put the dress on the child then slip on the cuffs over the sleeves as shown in diagram 6. Sew the narrow end of the cuffs to the sleeves as shown in the diagram. Turn the wrist edges of the cuffs right back and catch to the velvet sleeves with a few stitches at the position shown in diagram 6.

Sash

Materials required to fit any size

46 cm (½ yd) of 92 cm (36 in.) wide thin fabric such as nylon chiffon.
2 large beads.
Scraps of narrow braid.

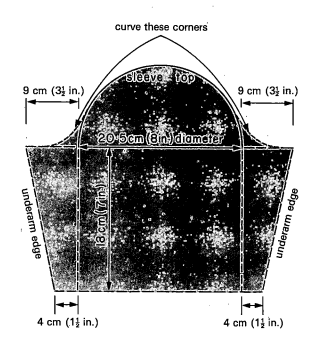

4. *Making the sleeve pattern.*

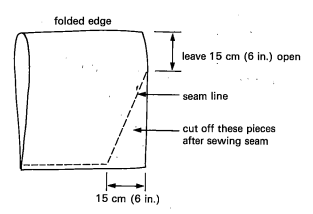

5. *Sewing the cuff seam.*

71

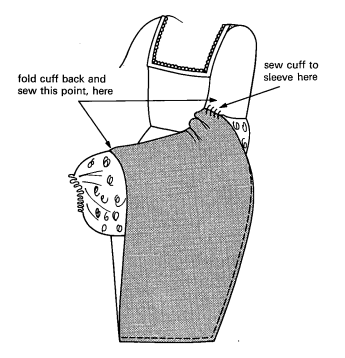

fold cuff back and
sew this point, here

sew cuff to
sleeve here

6. *Fixing the cuff to the sleeve.*

To make

Cut the fabric into two 23 cm by 92 cm (9 in. by 36 in.) strips. Join them together along one 23 cm (9 in.) edge to make one long strip. Join the long raw edges of the strip then turn right side out. Try the sash on the child tying it in a single loop as shown in the illustration. Cut the sash to the correct length if it is too long.

Slip a bead about 13 cm (5 in.) inside each end of the sash and tie a thread round the fabric on either side of the bead to hold it in place. Sew a scrap of braid round the fabric on either side of the bead. Hem the raw edges at the ends of the sash.

Gable head-dress

Materials required to fit any size

A rigid plastic hairband.
A 14 cm by 28 cm (5½ in. by 11 in.) strip of stiff white card.
70 cm (¾ yd) of narrow white tape.
46 cm (½ yd) of gold braid or trimming about 1.3 cm (½ in.) wide.
58 cm (⅝ yd) of 112 cm (44 in.) wide thin black fabric for the veil.
A 15 cm by 92 cm (6 in. by 36 in.) strip of brocade fabric.
Adhesive.

To make

Cut the card to the shape shown in diagram 7, then fold it along the lines marked 'fold' to make the gable shape. Curl up the extended ends of the gable as shown in diagram 8.

Place the plastic hairband 2.5 cm (1 in.) inside the face edge of the gable shape and stick it to the card where it touches at the positions shown in diagram 8. Allow the glue to dry. Cut the tape in two pieces and sew one end of each tape round the hairband at each side as shown in the diagram, for tying under the chin.

For the veil, cut a 112 cm (44 in.) diameter semicircle of black fabric. Make a 25.5 cm (10 in.) cut in the veil as shown in diagram 9, then hem all the raw edges. Place the straight edge of the veil over the back part of the gable shape and stick in place as indicated in diagram 7 so that the veil will hang down the back.

For the ornamental band, join the long raw edges and across one short end of the strip of brocade fabric. Turn right side out and press then turn in and slip stitch the remaining raw edges. Place the band on the front portion of the gable shape to cover the card having the ends hanging down equally at each side. Stick the band in place but do not stick it to the curled-up pieces of card. Fold the long ends of the band back up towards the

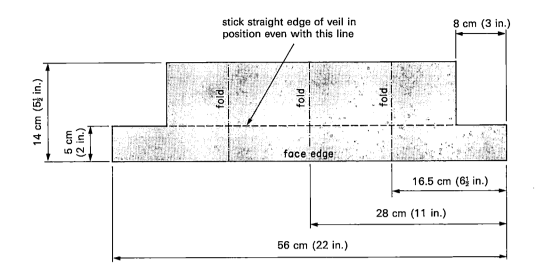

stick straight edge of veil in position even with this line

8 cm (3 in.)

14 cm (5½ in.)

5 cm (2 in.)

fold

fold

fold

face edge

16.5 cm (6½ in.)

28 cm (11 in.)

56 cm (22 in.)

7. *The pattern for the gable head-dress.*

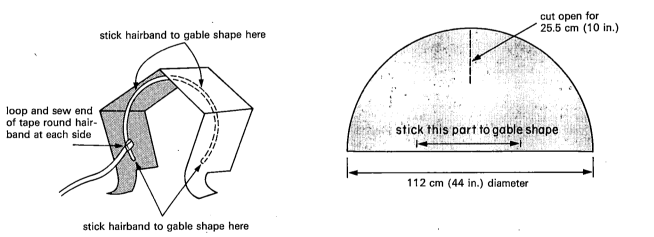

stick hairband to gable shape here

loop and sew end of tape round hair-band at each side

stick hairband to gable shape here

cut open for 25.5 cm (10 in.)

stick this part to gable shape

112 cm (44 in.) diameter

8. *Sticking the hair band inside the gable shape.*

9. *Cutting the veil.*

centre top of the head-dress and pin them there. One side of the veil can also be looped up at the back and pinned in this position leaving the other side hanging down as shown in the black and white illustration.

Finally stick the braid at right angles to the front edge of the head-dress as illustrated, clipping it at the corners to fit.

Underskirt

Make in the same way as given for the Victorian evening dress underskirt.

Hairstyle

The hair should be parted in the centre at the front and pinned up to be hidden by the head-dress.

Jewellery

As many finger rings as desired may be worn. Plain beads or strings of pearls can be sewn in loops to the bodice front as shown in the illustration. Thin silky gold cord is used here for the neck 'chains' with a brooch sewn to one of them for a pendant.

Aladdin

This fancy dress is suitable for a boy or girl using an ordinary pair of pyjamas as a basis. The magic lamp can be made from an old gravy or sauce boat.

Shirt and pants

For these, use a pair of pyjamas, if possible a size or two larger than the child would normally wear so that the legs of the pants will hang in baggy folds around the ankles. Run a tacking thread along the inside of each of the pyjama sleeves parallel with the seams to make the sleeves fit tightly to the wrists. The tacking threads can be removed later. The pyjama top should be worn back to front.

Shoes

Use black slip-on gym shoes, gluing a strip of 2 cm ($\frac{3}{4}$ in.) wide white elastic round the soles as shown in the illustration.

Wig

Materials required to fit any size

A piece of black knitted-type fabric, for example black brushed nylon or wool jersey, measuring 30.5 cm by 61 cm (12 in. by 24 in.).
Short length of narrow elastic.

To make

Cut an 18 cm (7 in.) wide strip of the fabric long enough to go around the child's head plus 2.5 cm (1 in.). Run a gathering thread along the centre of the strip parallel to the short edges, pull up the gathers to measure 9 cm ($3\frac{1}{2}$ in.) and fasten off. This forms the centre parting on the wig. Join the 18 cm (7 in.) edges. Hem the remaining raw edges and thread the elastic through one hem to gather up the fabric for the crown of the head.

For the plait, cut three long strips of fabric from the remaining piece and plait them together, cutting the ends to points to taper the plait towards its end. Tie black thread round the end of the plait. Sew the top end of the plait to the centre back of the wig. When the wig is worn, tuck the child's own hair out of sight beneath it.

Tunic and hat

Materials required for height 142 cm (4 ft 8 in.)

1.9 m (2 yd) of 122 cm (48 in.) wide brocade curtain fabric.
2.5 m ($2\frac{3}{4}$ yd) of braid for trimming the tunic.
Piece of stiff card for the hat shape 40.5 cm (16 in.) square.

Sticky tape.
46 cm (½ yd) of narrow black elastic for the hat.
92 cm (1 yd) of bobble braid for trimming the hat.
Adhesive.

To make the tunic

Use the tunic pattern as given on page 9. Try the pattern against the child to check that the lower edge is mid-thigh length and shorten or lengthen the pattern as necessary. Cut out the tunic from fabric, then cut out the V-neckline on the front only.

Join the underarm and side seams from the wrist edges only as far as the line marked A on the pattern in order to leave side slits. Clip the underarm curves. Try the tunic on the child to see if larger turnings need to be taken on these seams and also to check if the sleeve edges need to be shortened.

Turn the raw wrist and neck edges 0.6 cm (¼ in.) to the outside and stitch down, clipping the neck edge if necessary. Hem the lower edges and the side slits.

Stitch braid to the wrist edges to cover the raw edges of the tunic. Stitch braid around the neck edge, across to one side seam then down the side seam to the hem, easing the braid in to tucks around the curved neck edge to make it fit.

To make the hat

Make the basic hat shape from card using three-quarters of a 40.5 cm (16 in.) diameter circle as a pattern. Overlap the straight edges of the card about 5 cm (2 in.) at the outer edge, tapering up to the point. Hold this edge firmly in place with sticky tape.

Cut two pieces of brocade fabric using the basic three-quarter circle pattern, allowing 1.3 cm (½ in.) extra on the straight edges for seams and also 1.3 cm (½ in.) extra on the outer edges. Place the wrong side of one fabric shape on the outside of the hat and pin the straight edges together to make the fabric fit the hat smoothly. Sew the seam as pinned, trim the seam, then glue the wrong side of the fabric piece to the inside of the hat.

Pierce a hole for the elastic in each side of the hat about 10 cm (4 in.) down from the top point. Push the ends of the elastic through the holes to the outside of the hat and glue down the ends, adjusting the length of the elastic to suit the child.

Cover the outside of the hat with fabric in the same way as for the inside. Trim the remaining raw edges of the fabric level with the card, then glue on the bobble braid as illustrated.

The magic lamp

Materials

An old gravy or sauce boat.
Bits of braid, paper doyleys and a bottle cap for decorating the lamp.
Piece of thin card for covering the top of the lamp.
Gold and black enamel paint.
Adhesive.

To make

Cut a piece of card to cover in the top of the gravy boat leaving a rounded hole at the spout end. Glue the card in position then cover the join by gluing braid all round the top, round the spout and down the handle. Decorate the lamp by gluing on bits of paper doyley, strips of braid and a bottle cap to the top as illustrated.

Paint the entire lamp with gold enamel paint and leave to dry. To give an antique finish, go over the decorated parts of the lamp with black enamel paint. When this is dry, lightly brush over the black parts once more using gold paint.

Make-up

Use a black eyeliner pencil to give Aladdin's eyes and eyebrows a slant-eyed look.

Mary, Mary quite contrary

This outfit is made from pink cotton gingham fabric. The posy has small silver bells and cockle shells glued on to it. The 'pretty maids' in the rhyme could be portrayed by a few smaller children dressed in the same way as Mary but in a different colour.

Dress and hat

Materials required for height 142 cm (4 ft 8 in.)

2.8 m (3 yd) of 92 cm (36 in.) wide fabric.
6.4 m (7 yd) of lace edging for trimming the edges of the dress and hat.
23 cm (¼ yd) of 92 cm (36 in.) wide plain taffeta for the belt.
8 cm (3 in.) of Velcro or hooks and eyes for the belt fastening.
1.6 m (1¾ yd) of narrow elastic.

To make the dress

Use the tunic pattern given on page 9 altering it as follows: shorten the sleeve edges to the lines marked A, then cut out the neck edge along the line marked A. Lengthen the hem edge of the tunic to make it about 30.5 cm (12 in.) above floor level when tried against the child. There is no need to alter the width of the pattern because the elasticated waist and sleeves ensure that the dress will fit all sizes.

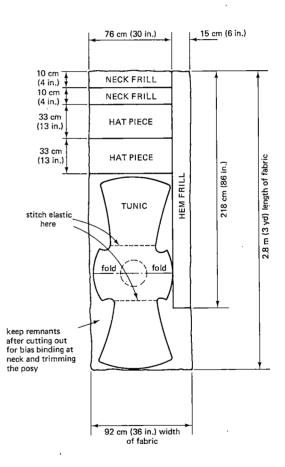

1. *Cutting out the dress and hat pieces.*

Cut out the tunic shape and all the other pieces for the hat and frills, etc as shown in diagram 1. Hem the sleeve edges then stitch on lace edging. Stitch a 20.5 cm (8 in.) length of elastic to the wrong side of each sleeve about 5 cm (2 in.) from the sleeve edges, stretching the elastic to fit as it is sewn on. Stitch two 30.5 cm (12 in.) lengths of elastic to the wrong side of the tunic almost level with the armholes as shown in diagram 1, stretching the elastic to fit as for the sleeves. Gather up the raw neck edge to measure 61 cm (24 in.) all round.

Join the side and underarm seams and clip the underarm curves. Join the short edges of the hem frill, then hem one long raw edge and stitch on lace edging. Gather up the other long raw edge to fit the lower edge of the tunic and stitch it in place. Join the short edges of the neck frill pieces, then hem and sew lace edging to one long raw edge. Gather up the other raw edge to fit the gathered neckline. Sew the frill to the neck edge with the raw edges even. Cut bias strips of fabric from remnants of the dress fabric and bind the raw neck edges.

For the belt, cut a 10 cm (4 in.) wide strip of taffeta long enough to go around the child's waist plus 8 cm (3 in.) for the back overlap. Narrowly hem all the raw edges, then press the strip into pleats along the length. Sew Velcro or hooks and eyes to the back edges then make a bow with the remaining piece of taffeta, having first hemmed all the raw edges. Sew the bow to one back edge of the belt.

To hold the belt in position, make belt carriers from loops of sewing thread just under the arms of the dress.

To make the hat

Join the two hat pieces together at two of the 33 cm (13 in.) edges. Hem and sew lace edging to one of the long edges. To the wrong side of the strip, stitch a 46 cm (18 in.) length of elastic parallel to and 10 cm (4 in.) from the lace trimmed edge, stretching the elastic to fit as it is sewn in place. Join the remaining short raw edges of the strip. Turn in the remaining long raw edge 0.6 cm ($\frac{1}{4}$ in.) and gather it up as tightly as possible, then fasten off the gathering thread.

The posy

Materials

Remnants of the dress fabric.
Small piece of card.
Scraps of green felt.
A few cockle shells.
A few silver bells.
Adhesive.

To make

Cut a 13 cm (5 in.) diameter circle of card and glue green felt to one side. On the green felt glue cockle shells, bells and green felt cut into leaf shapes. To the back of the posy, glue a tube of card covered with fabric for a handle, then glue a frill made from remnants of dress fabric round the edge of the posy.

Shoes, socks and gloves

Ballet shoes or slippers can be worn, sewing a small rosette of fabric to the front as illustrated. The socks and gloves are white.

Watering can

A plastic toy watering can completes the outfit.

Victorian evening dress c.1850

This pretty dress is easy to make using bris-bise net curtaining. This type of curtaining is made in widths of between 25.5 cm to 35.5 cm (10 in. to 14 in.) but alternatively, ordinary 122 cm (48 in.) wide net curtain fabric can be used, cut into narrow strips along the length. The bris-bise used for the dress illustrated is white and has a floral pattern in white and yellow.

A 'crinoline' shape can be achieved by making a very full underskirt using old cotton sheeting or any other available oddments of fabric.

Dress

Materials required for height 142 cm (4 ft 8 in.)

17.4 m (19 yd) of bris-bise net curtaining 35.5 cm (14 in.) in width, note that narrower widths can be used for smaller sizes.
3.5 m (3¾ yd) of 92 cm (36 in.) wide dress lining fabric such as satin or taffeta, the same colour as the net curtaining.
2.8 cm (3 yd) of wide ribbon.
46 cm (½ yd) of narrow elastic.
Hooks and eyes for the back fastening.

To make

For the basic skirt, cut a 2.8 m by 92 cm (3 yd by 36 in.) strip of dress lining fabric. The 92 cm (36 in.) measurement is the waist to floor length of the skirt, for smaller sizes adjust this measurement accordingly.

Narrowly hem one long edge of the fabric for the hem edge of the skirt. Mark a line on the fabric parallel to the hem edge and 1.3 cm (½ in.) less than the width of the bris-bise away from it as shown in diagram 1. Cut a 5.5 m (6 yd) length of bris-bise and gather the top edge to measure 2.8 m (3 yd). Sew the gathered edge in place on the skirt along the marked line.

For the top frill, cut a 2.8 m (3 yd) length of bris-bise. Sew the top edge of this to the top waist edge of the skirt, this edge is gathered up later on forming the frill.

For the middle frill, cut a 5.5 m (6 yd) length of bris-bise, gather the top edge to measure 2.8 m (3 yd). Mark the position of the top edge of this frill on the skirt between the other two frills taking care that the frills will overlap one another equally. Sew the frill in place.

Join the centre back edges of the skirt leaving a 15 cm (6 in.) gap at the top of the seam for the back opening. Press the seam to one side.

For the dress bodice, cut two strips of dress lining fabric and one strip of bris-bise to the sizes shown in diagram 2. Having the bris-bise between the two layers of lining fabric, join all the edges except for the waist edge. Turn right side out and press, then tack the waist edges together. The bris-bise is the right side of the bodice. From the remaining piece of lining fabric, cut two 30.5 cm

1. Marking the line for the first frill on the skirt.

2. The dress bodice.

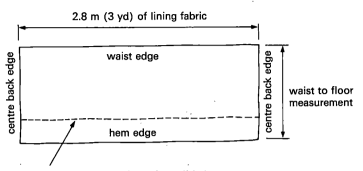

2.8 m (3 yd) of lining fabric

centre back edge | waist edge | centre back edge | waist to floor measurement

hem edge

mark line for first frill 1.3 cm (½ in.)
less than width of bris-bise away from it

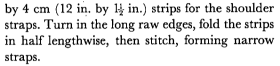

chest measurement plus 5 cm (2 in.)

centre back edge | top edge | centre back edge | underarm to waist measureme. plus 2. 5 cr (1 in.)

waist edge

by 4 cm (12 in. by 1½ in.) strips for the shoulder straps. Turn in the long raw edges, fold the strips in half lengthwise, then stitch, forming narrow straps.

Place the bodice inside out around the child, then overlap and pin the back edges to fit. Place a shoulder strap over each shoulder. Pin the ends of the straps to the bodice as shown in diagram 3, shortening them as necessary to make the bodice fit neatly under the arms. Now pin a dart in each side of the bodice through all thicknesses of fabric, from the waist edge tapering to the top edge as shown in diagram 3 to make the bodice fit neatly round the waist.

Take off the bodice, stitch the darts as pinned, then sew the ends of the straps in place.

For each sleeve, cut a 56 cm (22 in.) length of bris-bise. Thread a length of elastic through the casing in the top of each piece to fit the child's upper arm. Hold the ends of the elastic in place at each end with a few stitches. Join the short edges of each sleeve piece. Gather up the remaining edges to fit the armhole edges of the bodice. Sew the gathered edges in position on the shoulder straps and underarm of the bodice as shown in diagram 4.

Gather the top edge of the skirt to fit the lower edge of the bodice, then sew it in place. Sew hooks and eyes to the centre back overlap of the dress bodice.

3. Pinning on the shoulder straps and side darts.

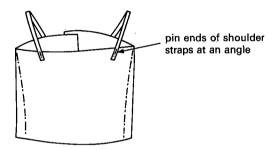

pin ends of shoulder straps at an angle

4. Sewing the sleeve in position.

84

For each shoulder piece, cut a strip of bris-bise long enough to reach from the back waist edge, over the shoulder to about 8 cm (3 in.) below the front waist edge.

Fold each piece along the length about three times to make strips about 13 cm (5 in.) in width. Turn in one short end of each strip 1.3 cm ($\frac{1}{2}$ in.) and run through a gathering thread pulling up the stitches to gather slightly. Sew these edges in place to the back waist edge of the bodice as shown in diagram 5.

Take the shoulder pieces over the shoulders toward the centre front and catch in place with stitches to the bodice as shown in diagrams 5 and 6. Pleat up the front ends of the shoulder pieces and sew the pleats in place. Sew the ends in place as shown in diagram 6. Sew on a ribbon bow to cover the ends of the shoulder pieces at the centre front, leaving loops of ribbon hanging down as illustrated.

Underskirt

Make this as full as possible according to the fabric available. A three-tiered skirt is best as shown in diagram 7 using 2.8 m (3 yd) for the top tier and adding more fullness to the second and third tiers. The gathered waist edge can be sewn to a length of tape leaving enough tape at each end for tying round the waist.

Hair

If the hair is long, it should be pinned up into a bun or coiled plaits. Ribbon bows, loops, artificial flowers are all suitable trimmings for pinning into the hair.

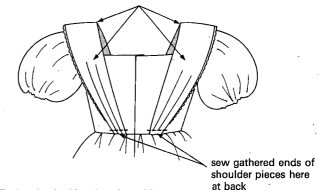

catch shoulder pieces to top of shoulder straps and top of bodice with a stitch here

sew gathered ends of shoulder pieces here at back

5. *Sewing the shoulder pieces in position at the back.*

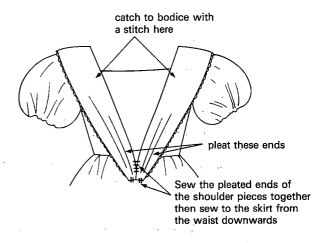

catch to bodice with a stitch here

pleat these ends

Sew the pleated ends of the shoulder pieces together then sew to the skirt from the waist downwards

6. *Sewing the shoulder pieces in position at the front.*

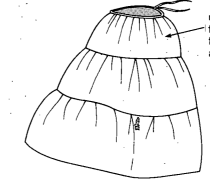

use about 2.8 m (3 yd) for the top tier and more fullness for the second and third tiers

7. *Making a three-tiered underskirt.*

85

Empire Costume c.1815

The very high waistline of this costume is characteristic of the period from about 1790 to 1820. Little short jackets called 'spencers' were worn and these just covered the dress bodices.

For this outfit a plain long sleeved T-shirt is used for the spencer and the dress skirt is attached to it. Spotted white curtain net with frilled edges is used for the skirt but white or pastel coloured cotton fabric with a small printed pattern would also be suitable. The pretty bonnet is covered in fawn fabric to look like straw and decorated with pink ribbons to match the spots on the dress.

Spencer

Use a long sleeved, high necked T-shirt or sweater in a dark colour.

Skirt, wrist and neck frills, puffed sleeves

Materials required for height 142 cm (4 ft 8 in.)

1.9 m (2 yd) of frilled edged curtain net 102 cm (40 in.) or more in width for the skirt.
The same amount of cotton or lining fabric for lining the skirt.
2.3 m (2½ yd) of 2.5 cm (1 in.) wide ribbon for the skirt band, wrist and neck bands and sleeve bands.
33 cm (13 in.) of Velcro.

58 cm (⅝ yd) of 92 cm (36 in.) wide fabric to match the T-shirt, for the puffed sleeves.

To make the skirt

First cut the frill off one long edge of the skirt fabric and sew it in position about 15 cm (6 in.) above the frill on the opposite edge. This double frilled edge will be the hem edge of the skirt and it can be decorated if desired with more frills and ruffles of ribbon.

Measure the correct skirt length on the child taking the measurements from the chest to just above the ankles. Trim a piece off the top edge of the skirt to make the skirt the correct length as shown in diagram 1.

Join the short edges of the skirt piece leaving 15 cm (6 in.) open at the top of the seam for the centre back opening of the skirt. Press the seam to one side.

Make the skirt lining in the same way as the skirt, omitting the frills and hemming the lower edge. Place the lining inside the skirt and tack the top raw edges together.

Cut a strip of ribbon long enough to go round the child's chest plus 5 cm (2 in.) for an overlap. Neaten the cut ends of the ribbon. Gather the top raw edges of the skirt to fit the ribbon strip, noting that about 25.5 cm (10 in.) should be left ungathered at the centre front of the skirt. Lap one long edge of the ribbon over the gathered top

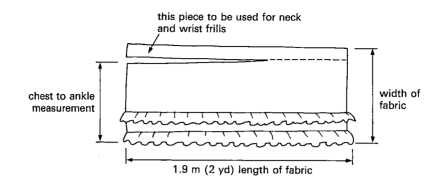

this piece to be used for neck and wrist frills

chest to ankle measurement

width of fabric

1.9 m (2 yd) length of fabric

1. *Cutting the skirt to the correct length.*

edges of the skirt and stitch in place. Sew 5 cm (2 in.) strips of Velcro to the ends of the ribbon where they overlap.

To make the skirt stay in the required high waisted position, strips of Velcro are sewn to the ribbon band and to the T-shirt. The Velcro strips can be removed if the T-shirt is to be used for ordinary wear later on.

Place the skirt on the child in the correct position on top of the T-shirt, then mark the position of the top edge of the ribbon band on the T-shirt at the centre front, under the arms and at each side at the back. Take off the T-shirt and sew on 4 cm (1½ in.) strips of the furry side of the Velcro at the marked positions. Sew the corresponding hooked strips of Velcro inside the ribbon band of the skirt at the centre front, sides and back.

To make the wrist and neck frills

Cut strips of ribbon long enough to go round the neck and each wrist, on top of the T-shirt, allowing 5 cm (2 in.) extra on each strip for neatening the ends of the ribbon and an overlap. Gather up narrow strips of the remaining skirt fabric and sew to the ribbon strips. Sew on 2.5 cm (1 in.) strips of Velcro at the overlaps.

To make the puffed sleeves

Make a pattern for the sleeves by drawing out a 51 cm (20 in.) diameter semicircle. Using this pat-

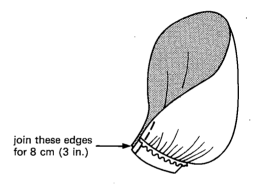

join these edges for 8 cm (3 in.)

2. *Joining the sleeve seam.*

tern, cut two sleeves from the fabric. Cut two strips of ribbon long enough to go round the child's upper arm plus 2.5 cm (1 in.), for the sleeve bands.

Gather the straight edges of the sleeves to fit the ribbon bands, then lap one long edge of each band over the gathered edge of the sleeve and sew it in place.

Fold each sleeve in half, bringing the ends of the ribbon bands together and join the raw edges of bands and sleeves for 8 cm (3 in.) as shown in diagram 2.

Turn the sleeves right side out and gather up the remaining raw edges to fit the armhole edges of the T-shirt. Slip each puffed sleeve over the T-shirt sleeves, turn in the gathered raw edges and slip stitch the sleeves in position. The puffed sleeves can be removed if the T-shirt is to be used for ordinary wear later on.

Bonnet

Materials required to fit any size

92 cm (1 yd) of 82 cm (32 in.) wide firm interlining for the bonnet shape.
70 cm (¾ yd) of 92 cm (36 in.) wide thin curtain net or cotton fabric for covering the bonnet shape.
Trimmings for the bonnet as available, ribbons or strips of curtain net, rosettes, artificial flowers, feathers etc.
1.6 m (1¾ yd) bias binding to match the bonnet fabric.
Adhesive.

To make

Cut two 15 cm (6 in.) wide strips of interlining long enough to go round the child's head plus 1.3 cm (½ in.). Glue the strips together. Cut one long edge of this strip in to a curved shape as shown in diagram 3. Overlap the 15 cm (6 in.) edges of the strip 1.3 cm (½ in.) and glue or sew in place forming a tube. The overlap will be at the centre back of the bonnet.

For the bonnet brim, cut two 30.5 cm (12 in.) diameter circles of interlining. Glue the circles together. Place the cut curved edge of the tube on to the bonnet brim a little off centre as shown in diagram 4. Mark the shape of the tube on to the bonnet brim. Carefully cut out the marked circle then place this small circle on to the top of the tube for the top of the bonnet. Oversew the edges of the tube and circle together as shown in diagram 5. This forms the completed crown of the bonnet.

To cover the bonnet crown, cut a 48.5 cm (19 in.) diameter circle of bonnet fabric. Run a gathering thread round the edge and place the circle over the bonnet crown, pulling up the gathers to fit inside the lower edge of the tube. Oversew the fabric to the tube at the lower edge.

To cover the brim of the bonnet, spread a little

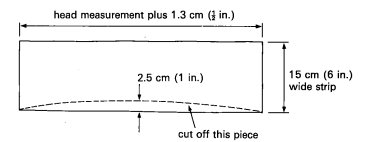

head measurement plus 1.3 cm (½ in.)

2.5 cm (1 in.)

15 cm (6 in.) wide strip

cut off this piece

3. *Cutting a curved piece off one edge of the bonnet strip.*

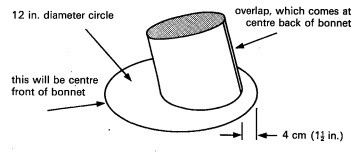

12 in. diameter circle

overlap, which comes at centre back of bonnet

this will be centre front of bonnet

4 cm (1½ in.)

4. *Placing the crown of the bonnet on the brim.*

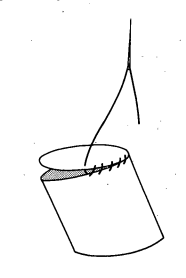

5. *Sewing the small circle to the top of the tube.*

adhesive round the outer and inner edges of the brim shape, then stick it on to a piece of the bonnet fabric. Cut out the fabric level with the interlining shape. Cover the other side of the brim with fabric in the same way. Bind the outer and inner edges of the brim with bias binding.

Place the bonnet crown in position on the brim as shown in diagram 4 and oversew the inner edge of the brim to the lower edge of the tube.

Attach a length of ribbon across the top of the bonnet slightly toward the back, so that the hat can be tied on under the chin bending down the brim at each side as shown in the illustration.

Trim the bonnet as desired. The bonnet illustrated has a ruffle of ribbon sewn to the inside edge of the brim. Strips of ribbon and net fabric are wound round the crown and made into rosettes and a few feathers are sewn on.

Socks and gloves

These can be white or pastel coloured.

Shoes

Use flat slippers or ballet shoes with a small ribbon bow sewn to the front of each one.

Hairstyle

Short hair can be formed into little ringlets on the forehead and the back will be hidden by the bonnet. Long hair should be parted in the centre and pinned in a bun on top of the head which will fit inside the crown of the bonnet.

Puss in Boots

Puss wears a dashing Cavalier style outfit. This costume is best suited to small children and can be worn by a boy or girl. While a pair of ordinary trousers or pyjama pants can be used, the pants illustrated are easy to make using striped curtain fabric.

Mask, paws and tail

Materials required to fit any size

35 cm ($\frac{3}{8}$ yd) of 122 cm (48 in.) wide black fur fabric.
70 cm ($\frac{3}{4}$ yd) of black, round elastic.

To make

For the mask cut two 25.5 cm by 28 cm (10 in. by 11 in.) pieces of fur fabric. On one piece cut out the holes for the mouth and eyes at the positions shown in diagram 1. Now join the two pieces of fur fabric round three edges taking 0.6 cm ($\frac{1}{4}$ in.) seam, leaving the lower 28 cm (11 in.) edges open and rounding off the upper corners as shown in the diagram. Trim off the excess fabric at the corners and turn right side out. Run a 30.5 cm (12 in.) length of elastic round the lower edge and knot the ends together.

Cut out four ear pieces to the size shown in the diagram. Join them in pairs taking 0.6 cm ($\frac{1}{4}$ in.)

seam and leaving the lower 10 cm (4 in.) edges open. Turn the ears right side out and oversew the raw edges together, pulling the stitches tightly to gather slightly. Sew the gathered edges of the ears in position as shown in the diagram.

For each paw, cut two 10 cm by 20.5 cm (4 in. by 8 in.) strips of fur fabric. Join them in pairs taking 0.6 cm ($\frac{1}{4}$ in.) seam, leaving one 10 cm (4 in.) edge open in each pair and rounding off all other corners. Trim off the corners and turn the paws right side out. Make two loops from the round elastic and wear these on the wrists on top of the paws to hold them in position.

For the tail cut a 6.5 cm by 33 cm ($2\frac{1}{2}$ in. by 13 in.) strip of fur fabric and cut the strip to a point at one end for the end of the tail. Oversew the long edges together with the right side of the fabric outside.

Pants

Materials required to fit any size

92 cm (1 yd) of 122 cm (48 in.) wide striped curtain fabric.
70 cm ($\frac{3}{4}$ yd) of 2.5 cm (1 in.) wide elastic.

To make

Cut out and make the pants as in the instructions on page 11. Sew the top end of the tail to the back

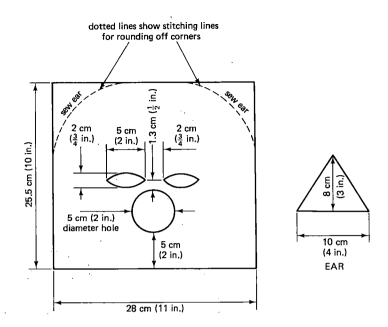

dotted lines show stitching lines
for rounding off corners

sew ear

2 cm
($\frac{3}{4}$ in.)

5 cm
(2 in.)

1.3 cm ($\frac{1}{2}$ in.)

2 cm
($\frac{3}{4}$ in.)

sew ear

25.5 cm (10 in.)

5 cm (2 in.)
diameter hole

5 cm
(2 in.)

28 cm (11 in.)

8 cm
(3 in.)

10 cm
(4 in.)

EAR

1. *Patterns for mask.*

of the pants about 20.5 cm (8 in.) down from the waist edge.

Lacy shirt

Trim a white school shirt or blouse with gathered ruffles of lace trimming tacked to the collar, cuffs and down the centre front. As an economical substitute for lace trimming, 23 cm ($\frac{1}{4}$ yd) of lacy curtain net cut into strips and gathered will do very well.

Boots

Black wellington boots are used, making the turn-over tops from leatherette or felt.

Materials

A piece of black leatherette or felt 35.5 cm (14 in.) square.

Adhesive (use a rubberized adhesive if the tops are to be removed later).

To make

For the turn-over tops make a paper pattern as follows: draw out a 35.5 cm (14 in.) diameter circle, cut it out, then draw an 18 cm (7 in.) diameter circle in the centre of the 35.5 cm (14 in.) diameter circle, cut it out and discard it. Cut the remaining pattern piece in half and using one half as a pattern, cut out two pieces from leatherette or felt.

Fit the inner curved edge of each piece about 1.3 cm ($\frac{1}{2}$ in.) inside the top edge of each boot, overlapping and pinning the short straight edges together at the backs of the boots as necessary to fit. Remove the tops, then sew the overlapped edges together as pinned, cutting off any excess. Glue the inner curved edges 1.3 cm ($\frac{1}{2}$ in.) inside the tops of the boots.

Cape

Materials required to fit any size

1.2 m (1¼ yd) of 122 cm (48 in.) wide curtain fabric.
4.6 m (5 yd) of narrow braid or bias binding.

To make

Make a paper pattern for the cape as follows: draw and cut out a 112 cm (44 in.) diameter circle with a 13 cm (5 in.) diameter circle cut out of the centre for the neck edge. Cut away one quarter of the circle altogether and discard it. Use the remaining three-quarter circle as a pattern.

Cut out the cape and either bind the raw edges with bias binding or turn and press them 0.6 cm (¼ in.) to the outside of the cape, clipping the neck curve, and stitch on braid to cover the raw edges. When binding the neck edge leave lengths of braid or bias at the centre front neck edges to use as ties.

Hat

Materials required to fit any size

46 cm (½ yd) of 122 cm (48 in.) wide plain fabric.
Two 40.5 cm (16 in.) squares of firm interlining.
1.4 m (1½ yd) of bias binding.
A few large feathers or bits of marabou feather trimming.
Adhesive.

To make

For the hat brim cut two 40.5 cm (16 in.) diameter circles from the squares of interlining and glue them together. Cut out a 16.5 cm (6½ in.) diameter circle from the centre and discard it. Spread a little glue round the outer and inner edge of the brim shape and then stick it on to the hat fabric. Cut out the brim level with the interlining shape at the centre and outer edges. Cover the other side of the interlining with fabric in the same way. Bind the outer edge of the brim with bias binding.

For the crown of the hat cut two 18 cm by 29 cm (7 in. by 11½ in.) strips of hat fabric. Join these pieces together at the 18 cm (7 in.) edges taking 0.6 cm (¼ in.) seams. Now stitch one of the long raw edges of the crown to the inner edge of the brim taking a 0.6 cm (¼ in.) seam. Trim the seam. Run a gathering thread along the remaining raw edge of the crown, pull up the gathers tightly and fasten off the thread.

Sew feathers to the hat brim as illustrated.

Belt

Any available belt can be used, or a belt can be made from a strip of leather cloth, attaching a buckle to one end.

Rapier or sword

A cheap plastic toy sword tucked into the belt completes the outfit.

A list of costumes in alphabetical order